Precious Animals

by

Angela Sciddurlo Rago

www.RenaissancePublisher.com

ISBN-13: 978-1541083097

Precious Animals is a collection of wild and not-so-wild animals indulging in beautiful settings and covered with precious jewelry.

All of these original pen drawn drawings are intentionally not vectored, giving you a drawing that is more natural and making your final artwork stand out as an original work of art that you can proudly frame.

Some of the drawings are more challenging than others, but with passion and love you can certainly complete them all.

For this reason, the drawings are presented in duplicate form. You can test your colors and technique in the (Work Area), and in the (Beauty Area) you can complete your masterpiece!

So, relax... and color your stress away!

Work Area

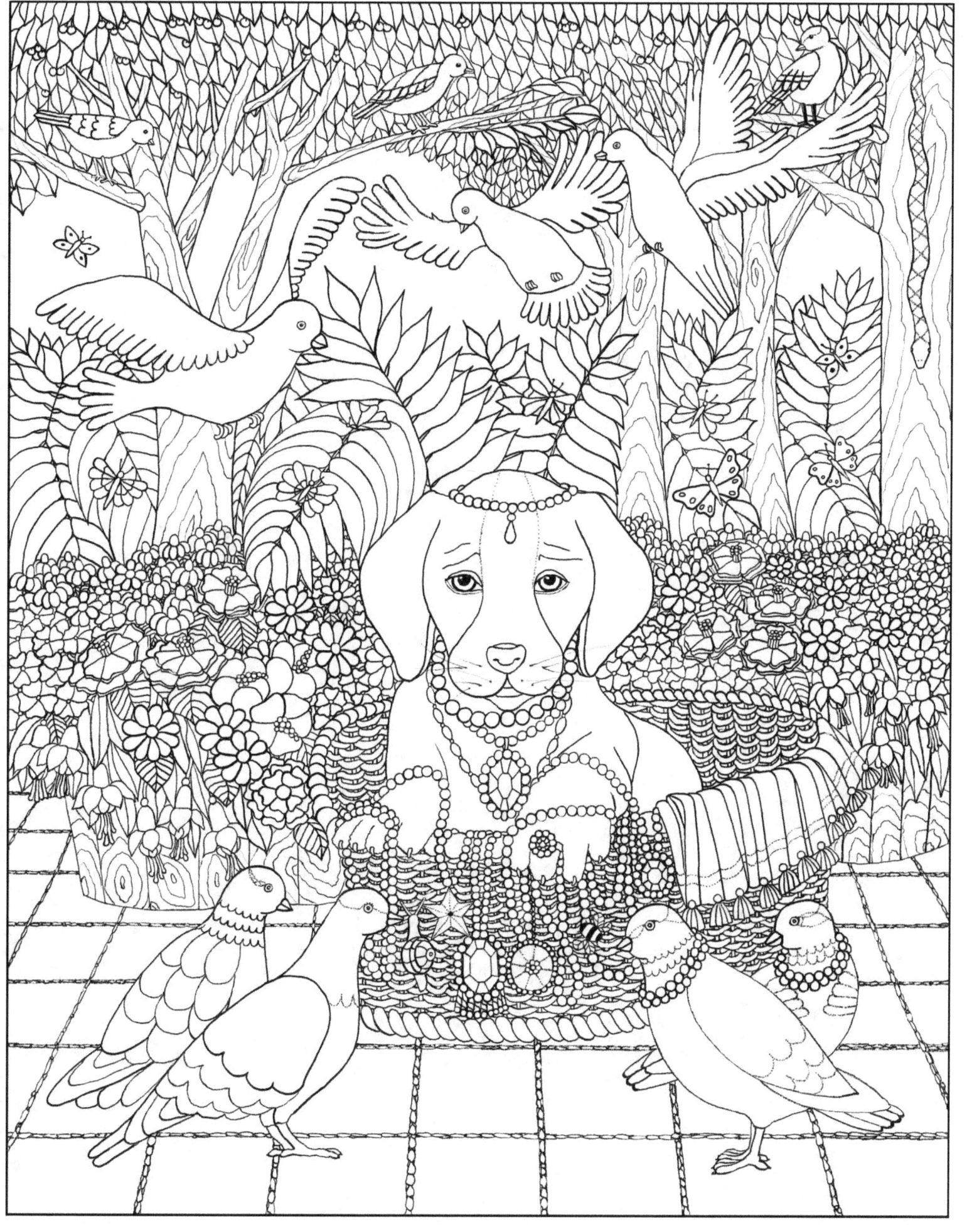

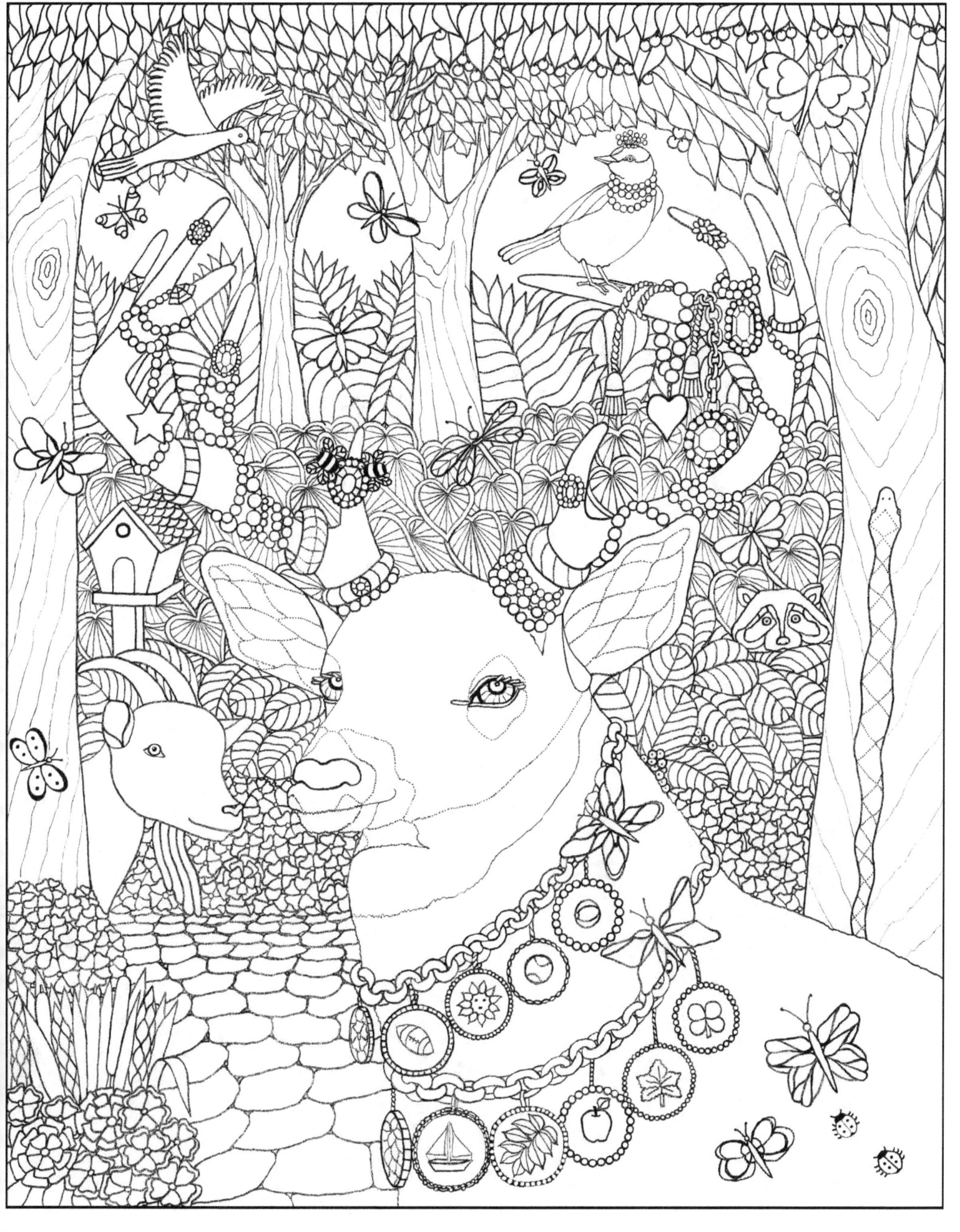

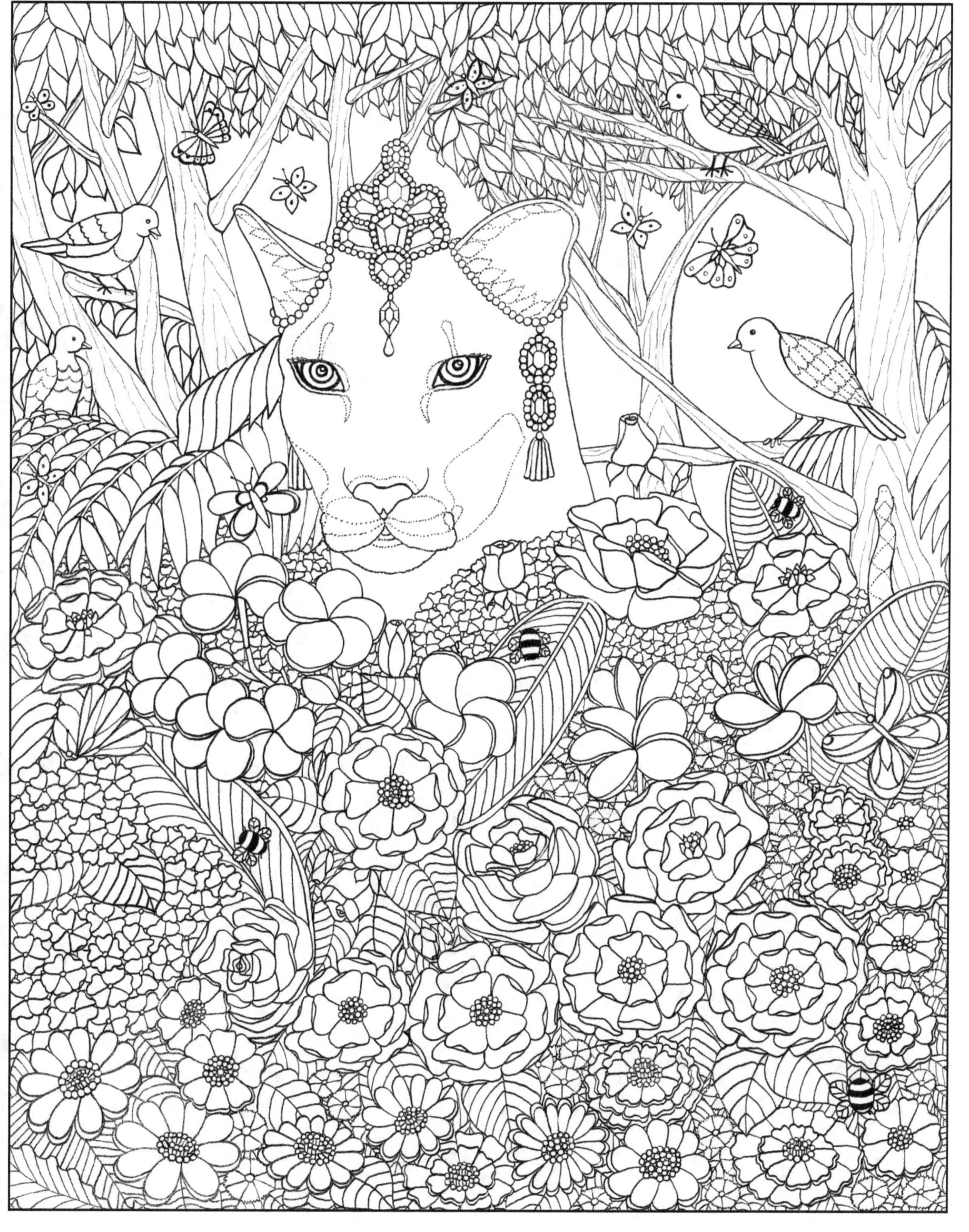

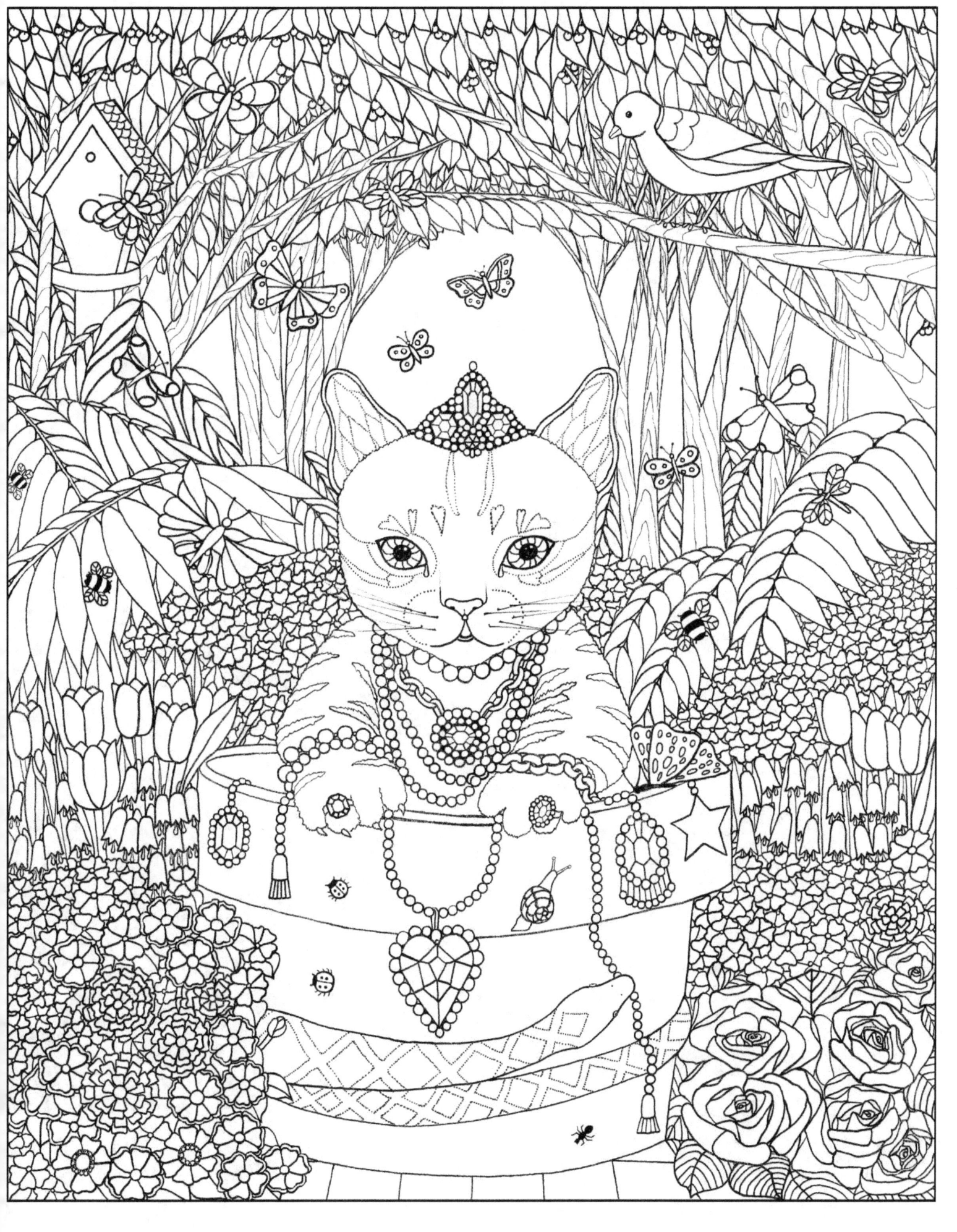

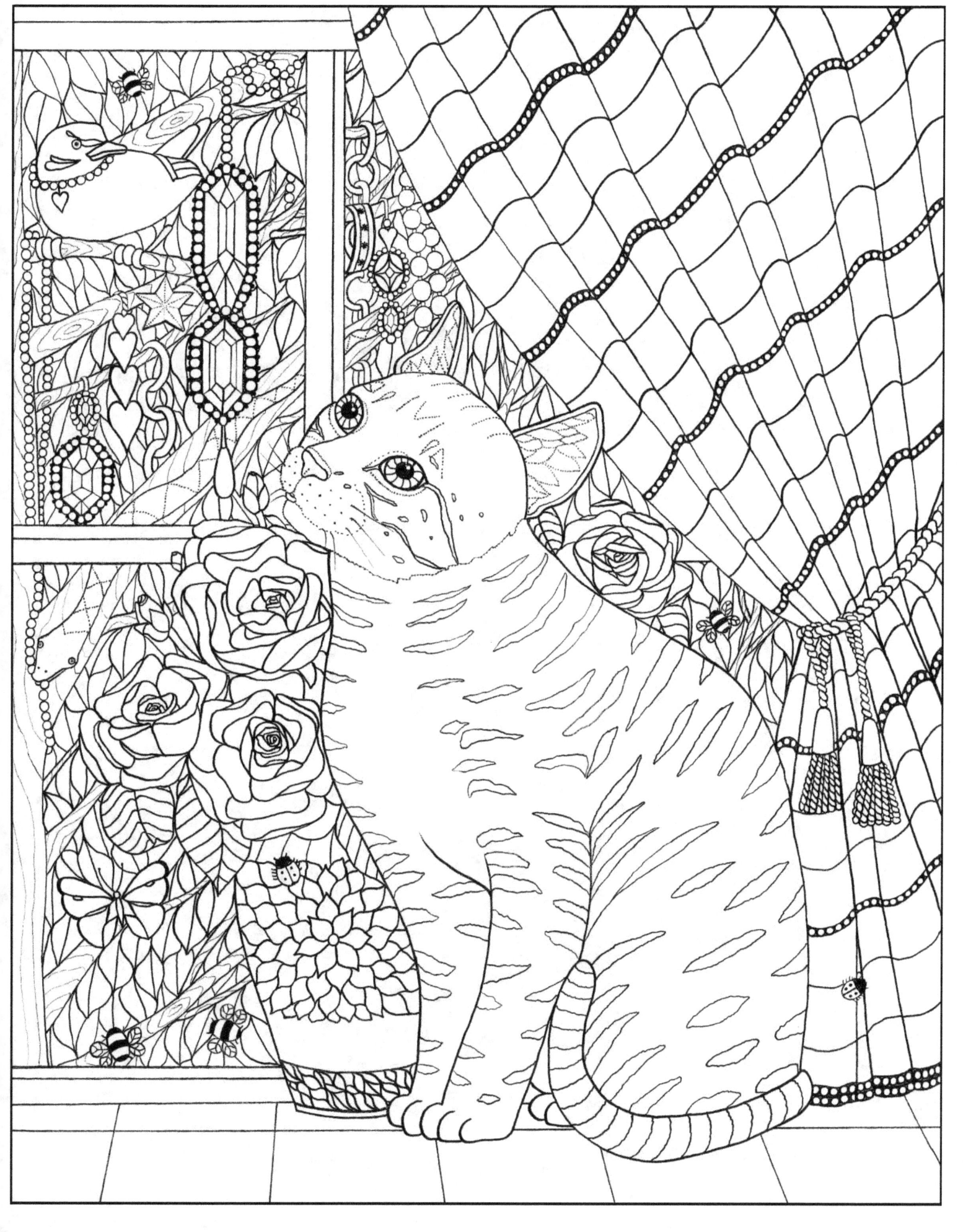

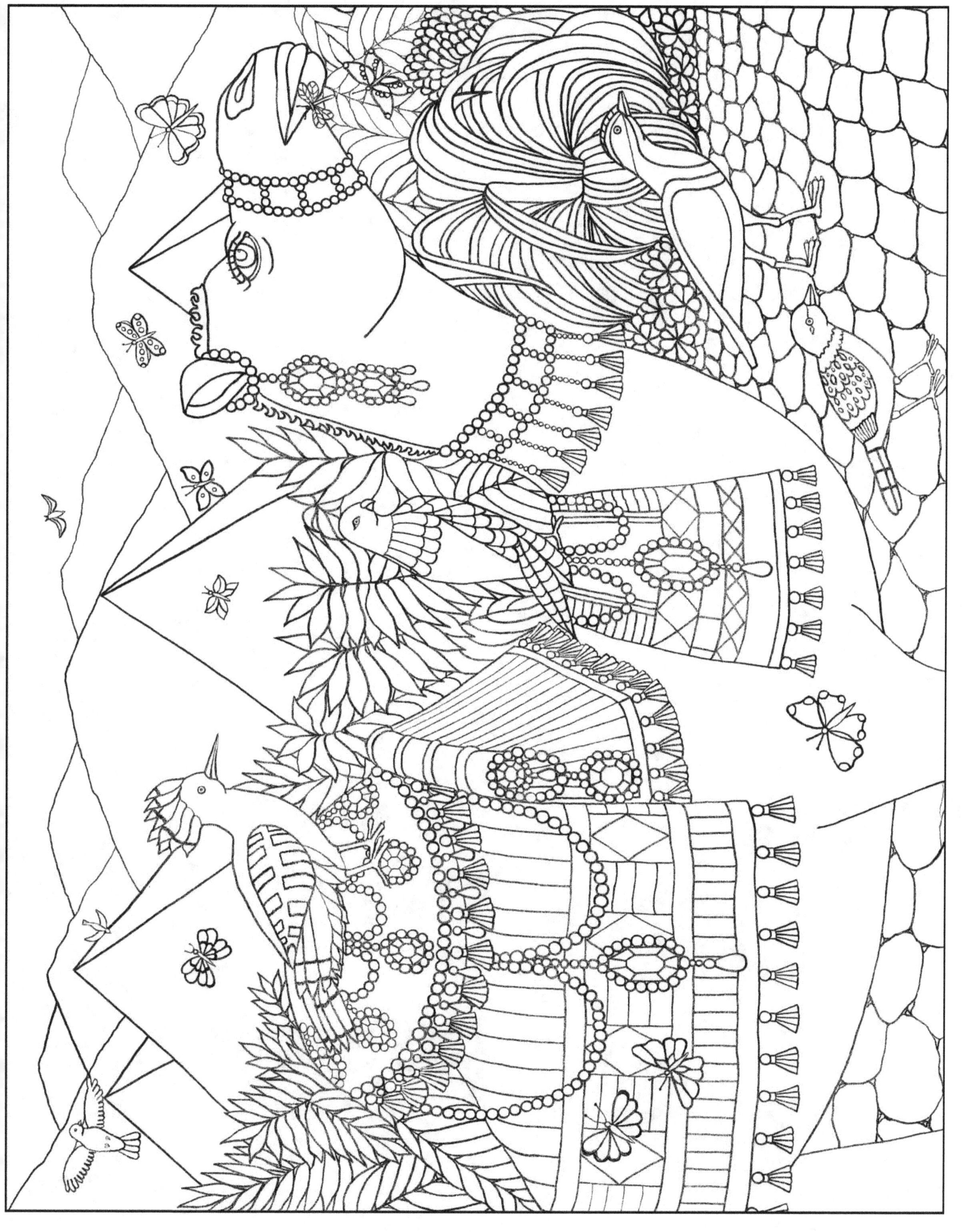

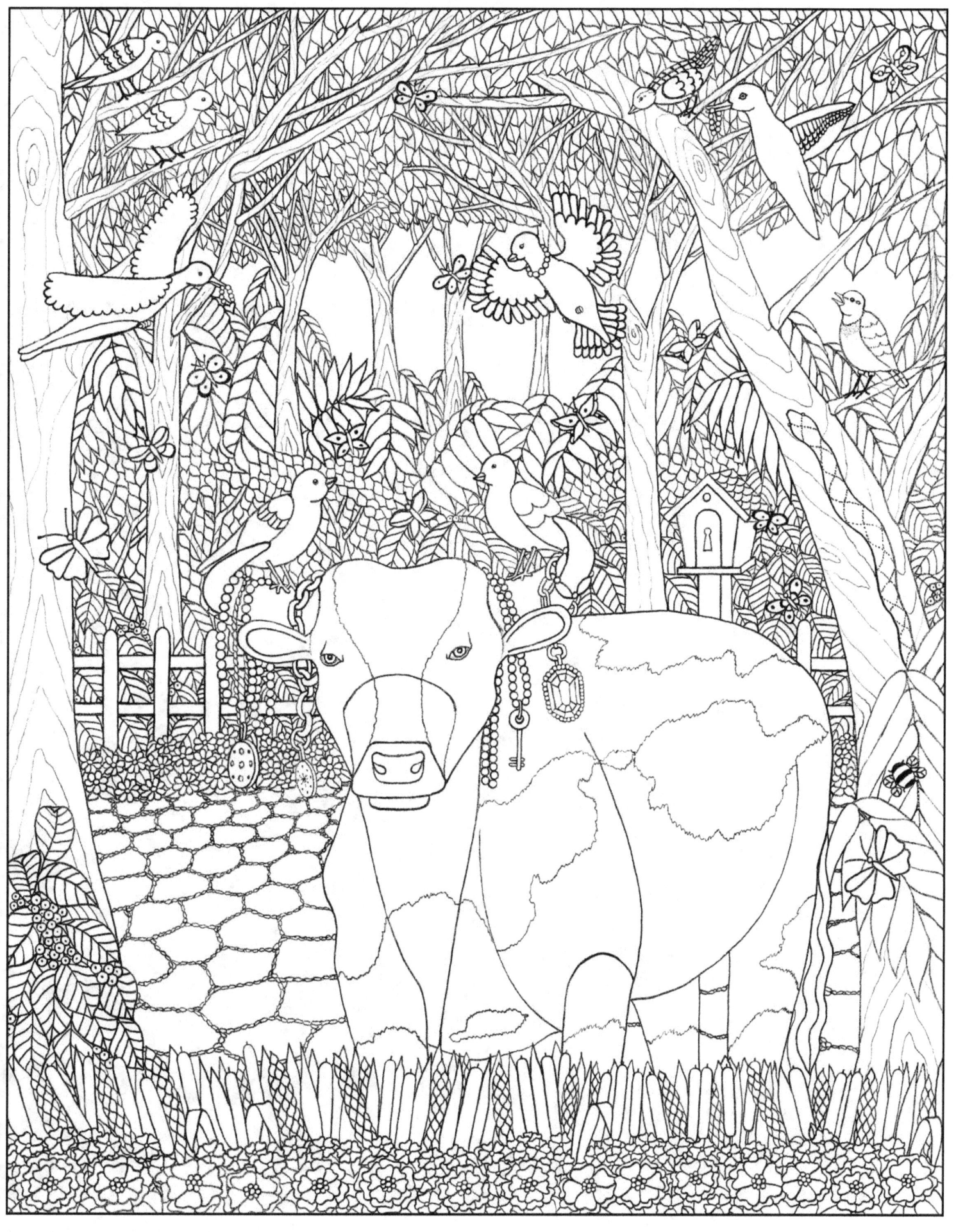

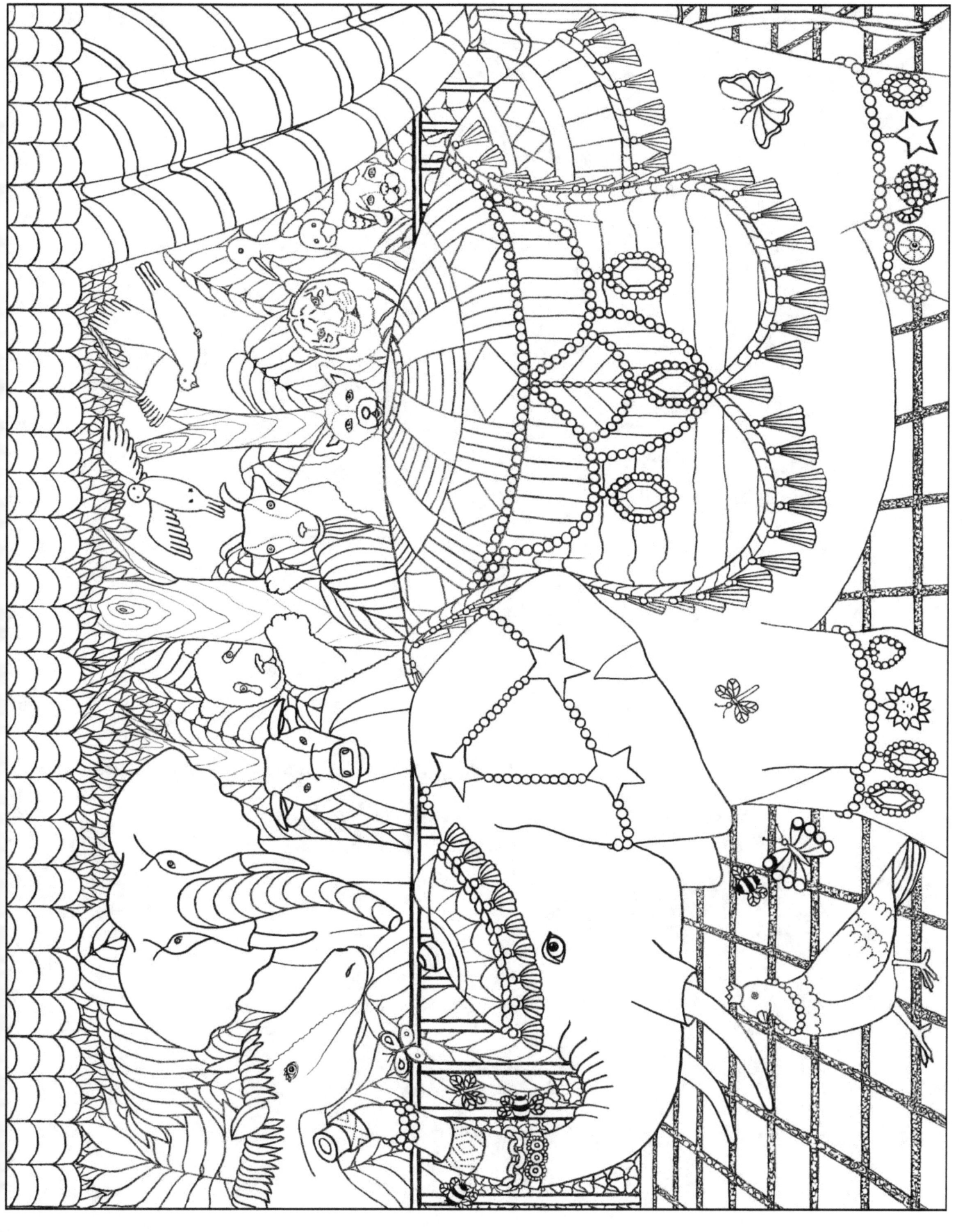

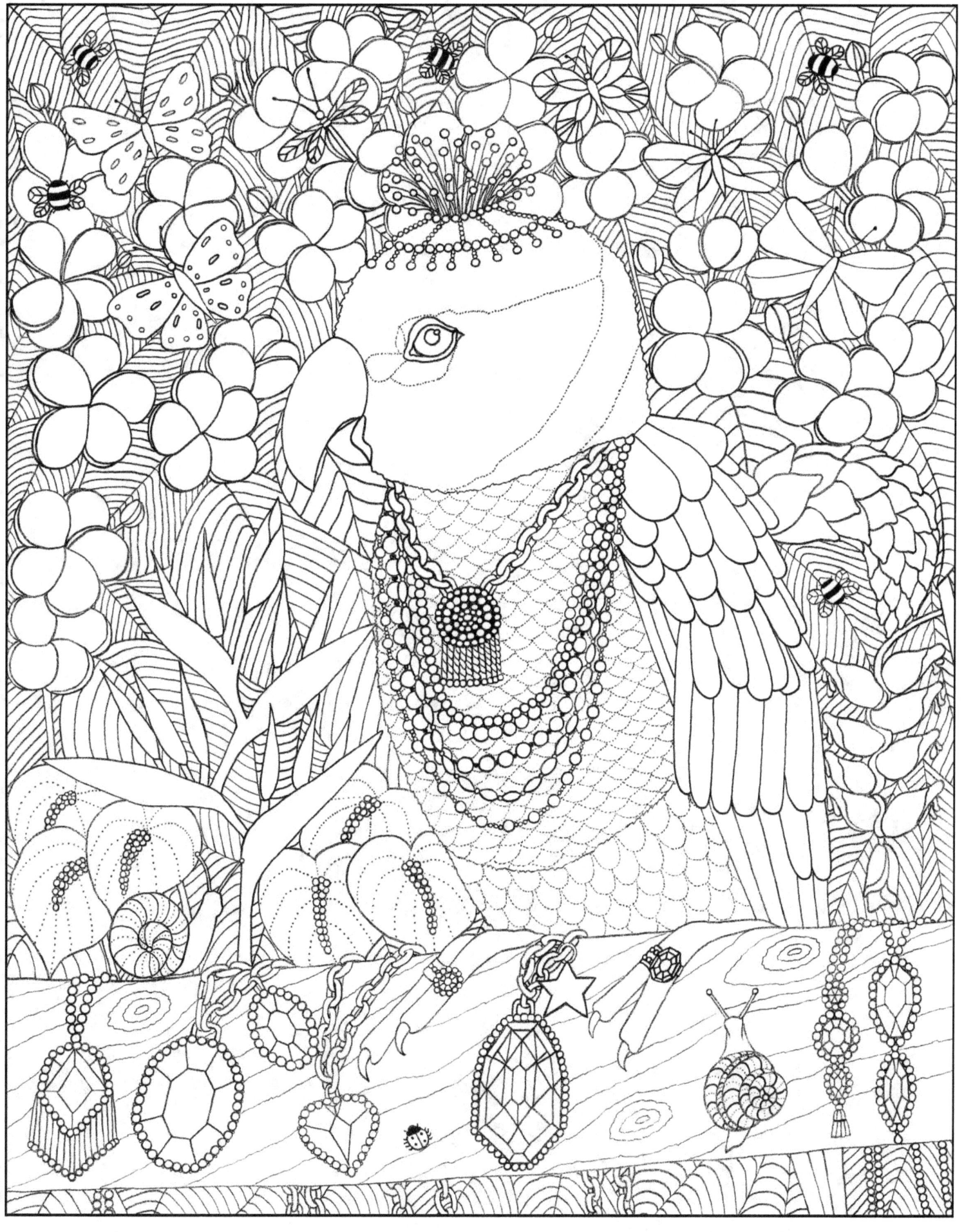

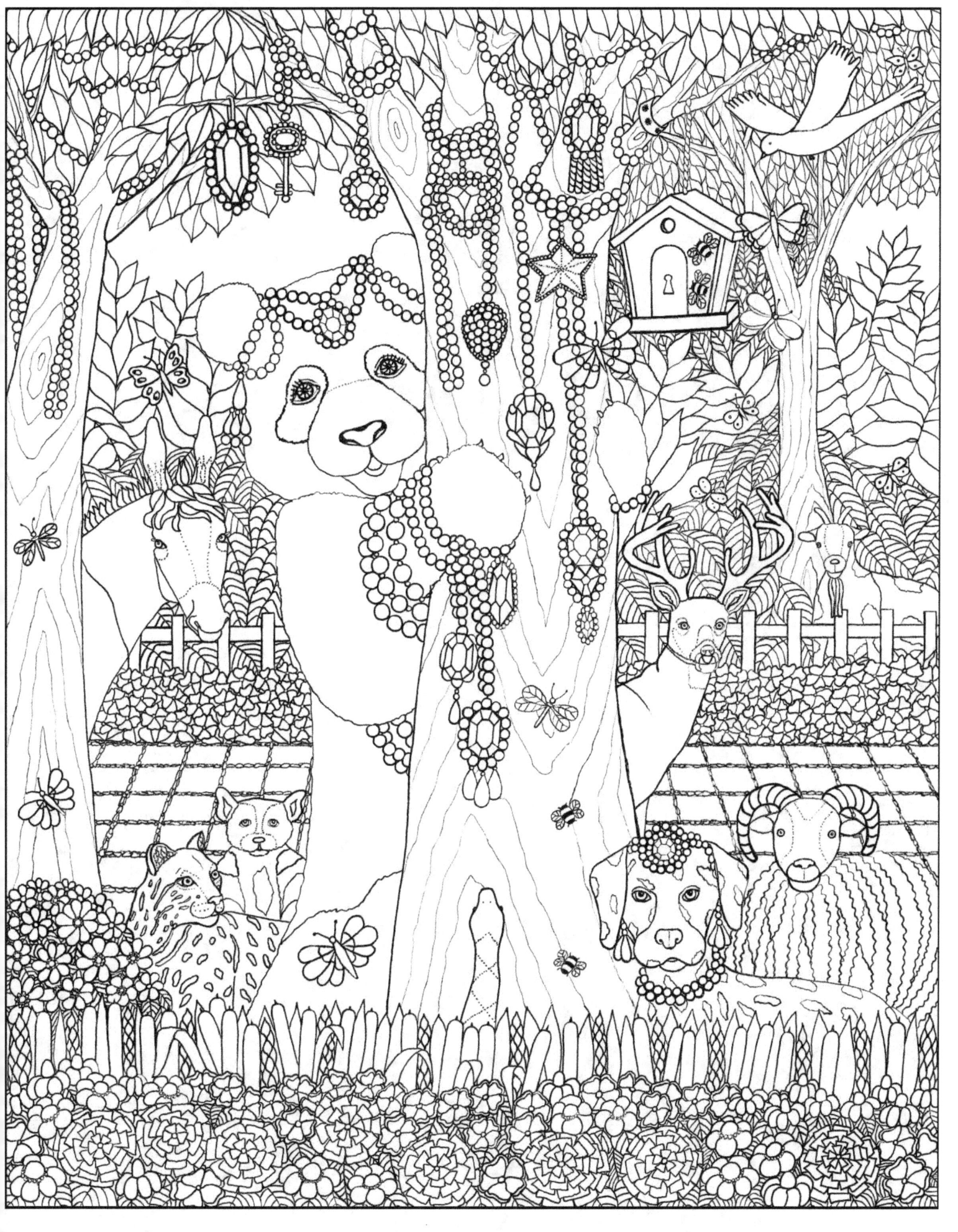

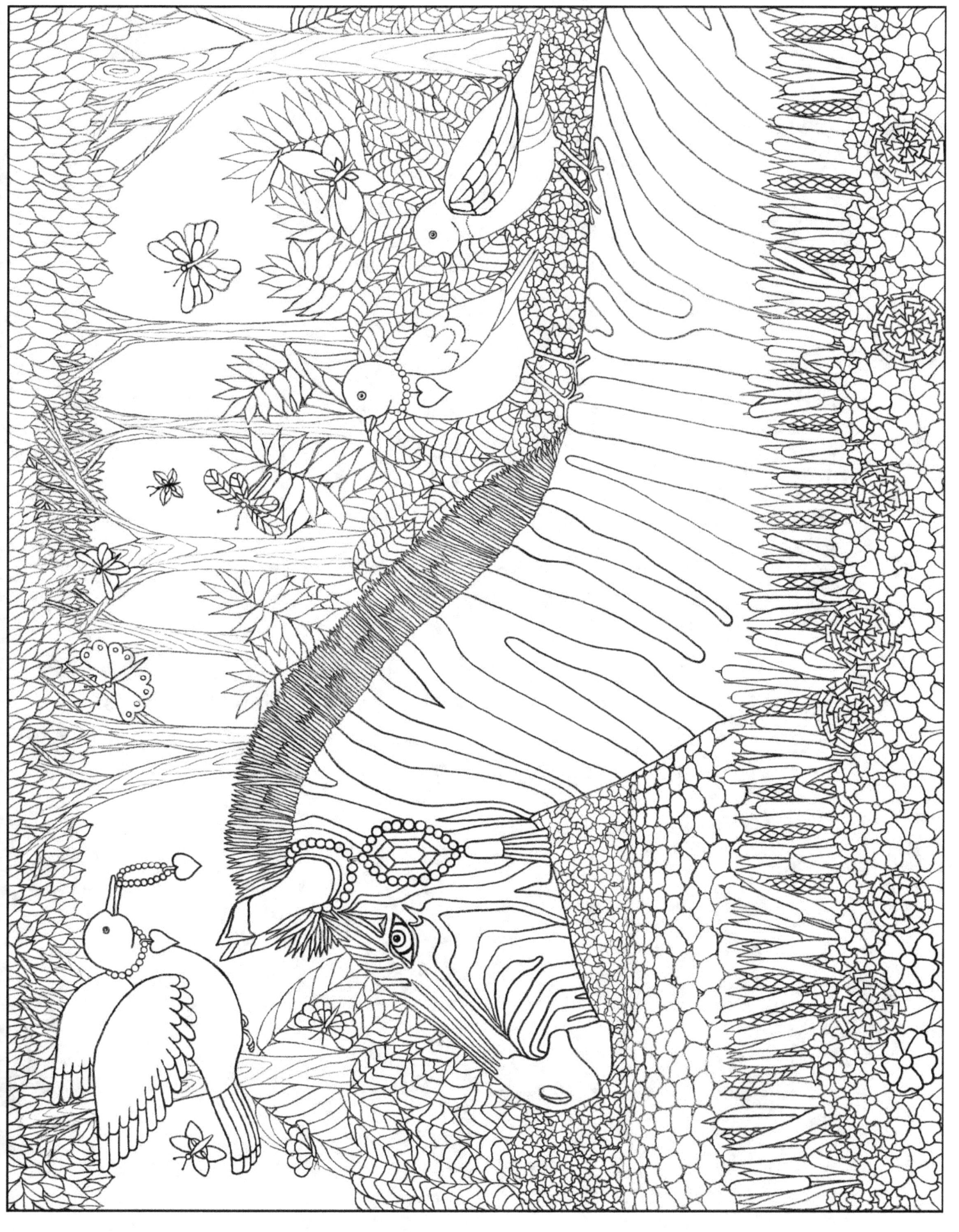

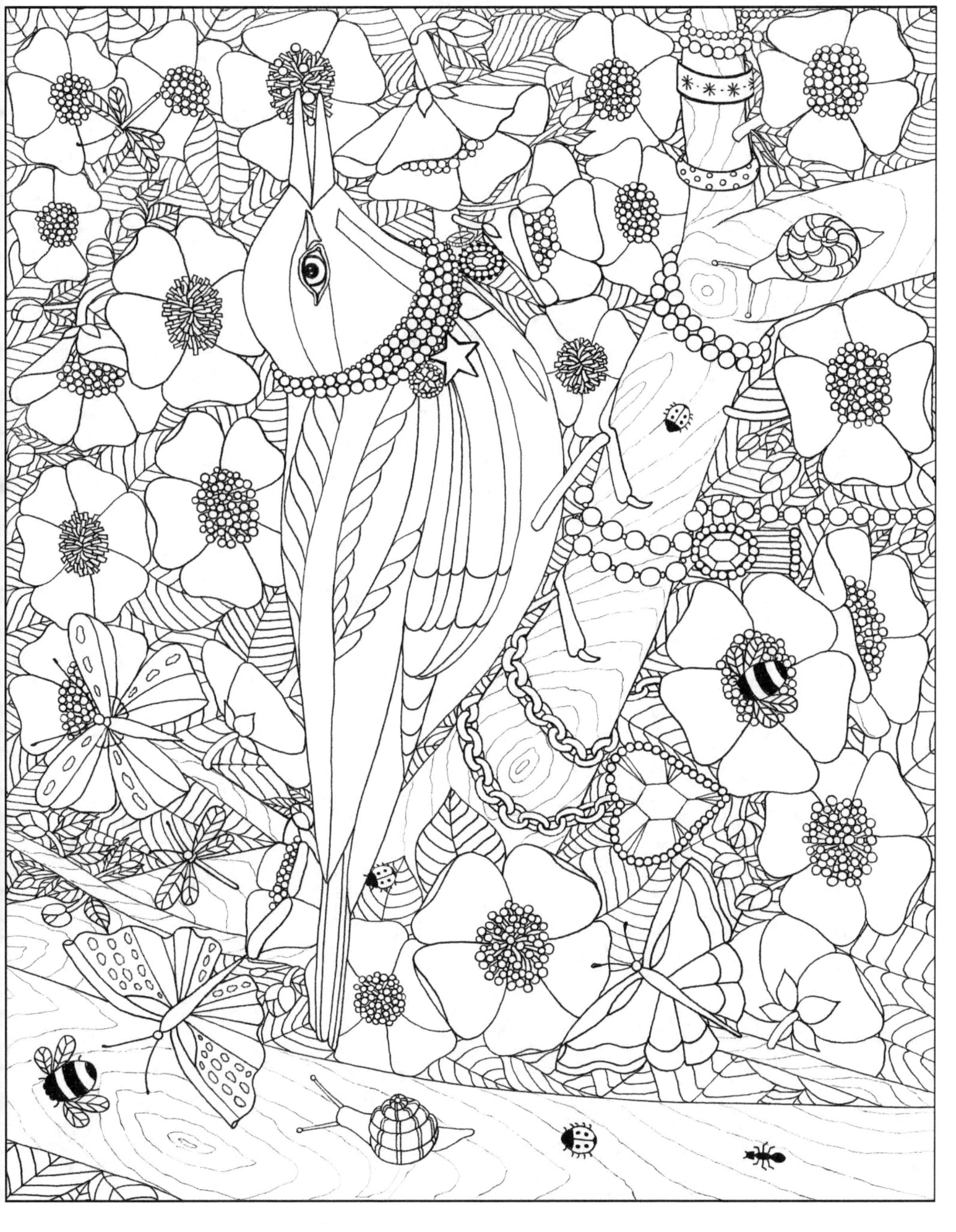

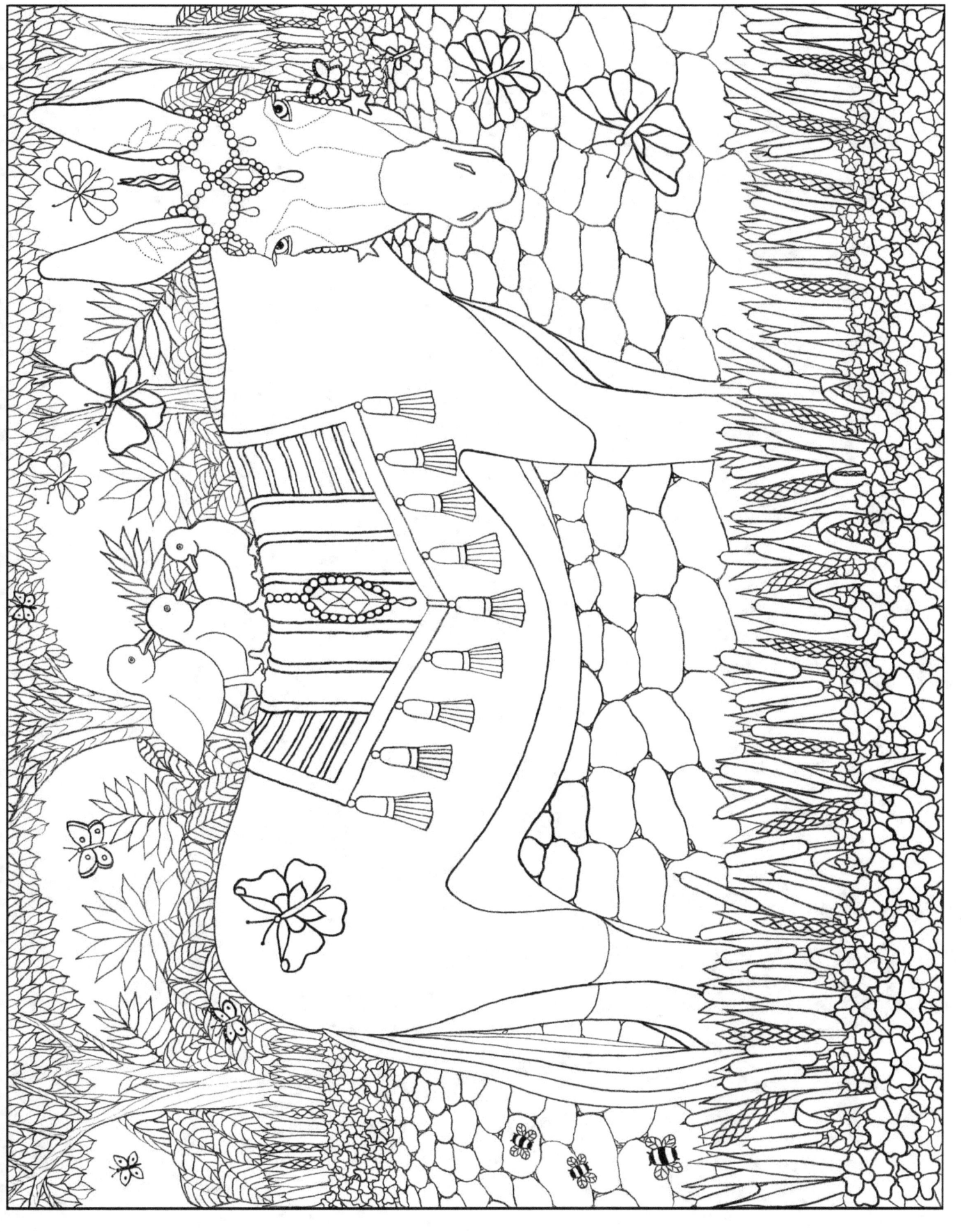

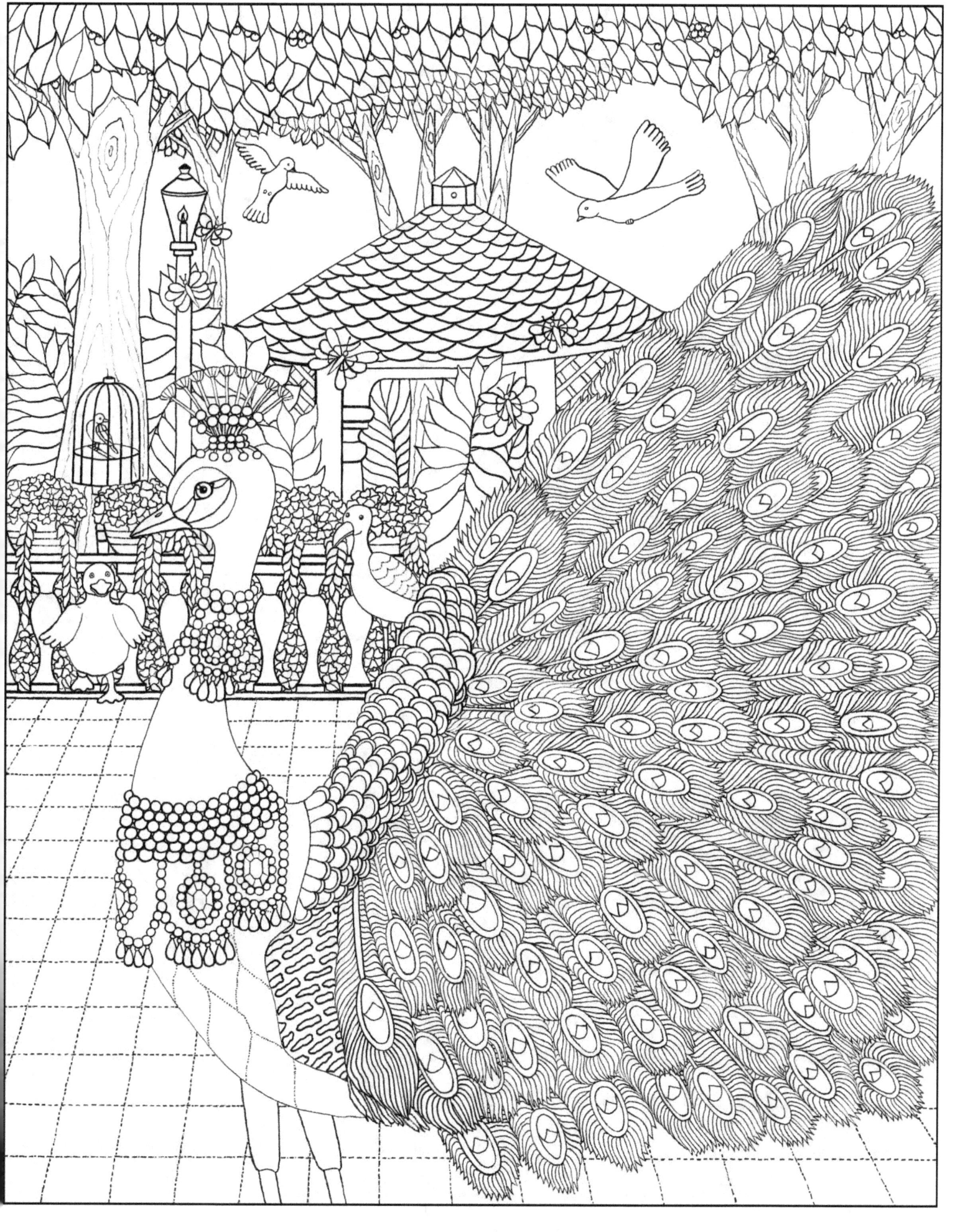

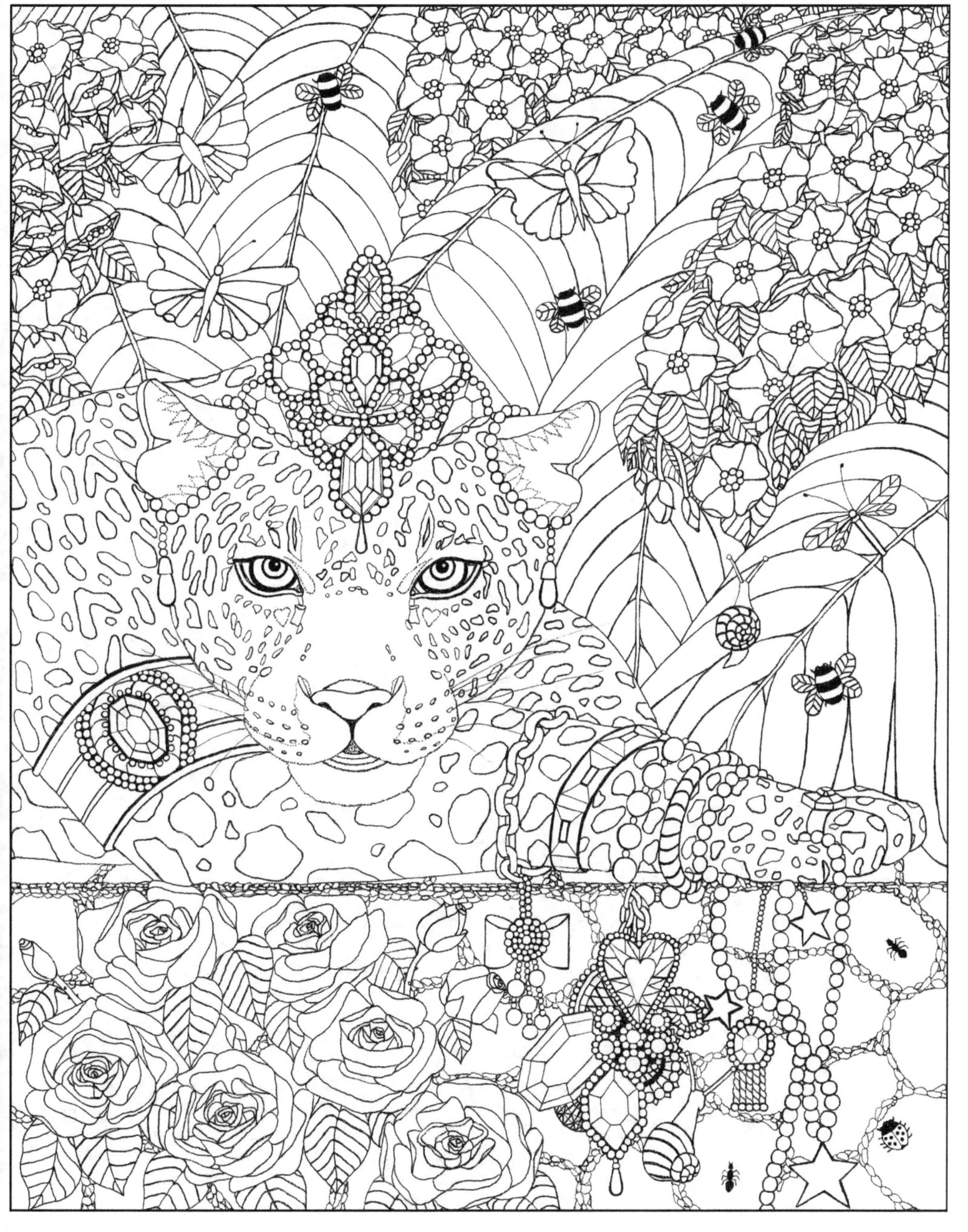

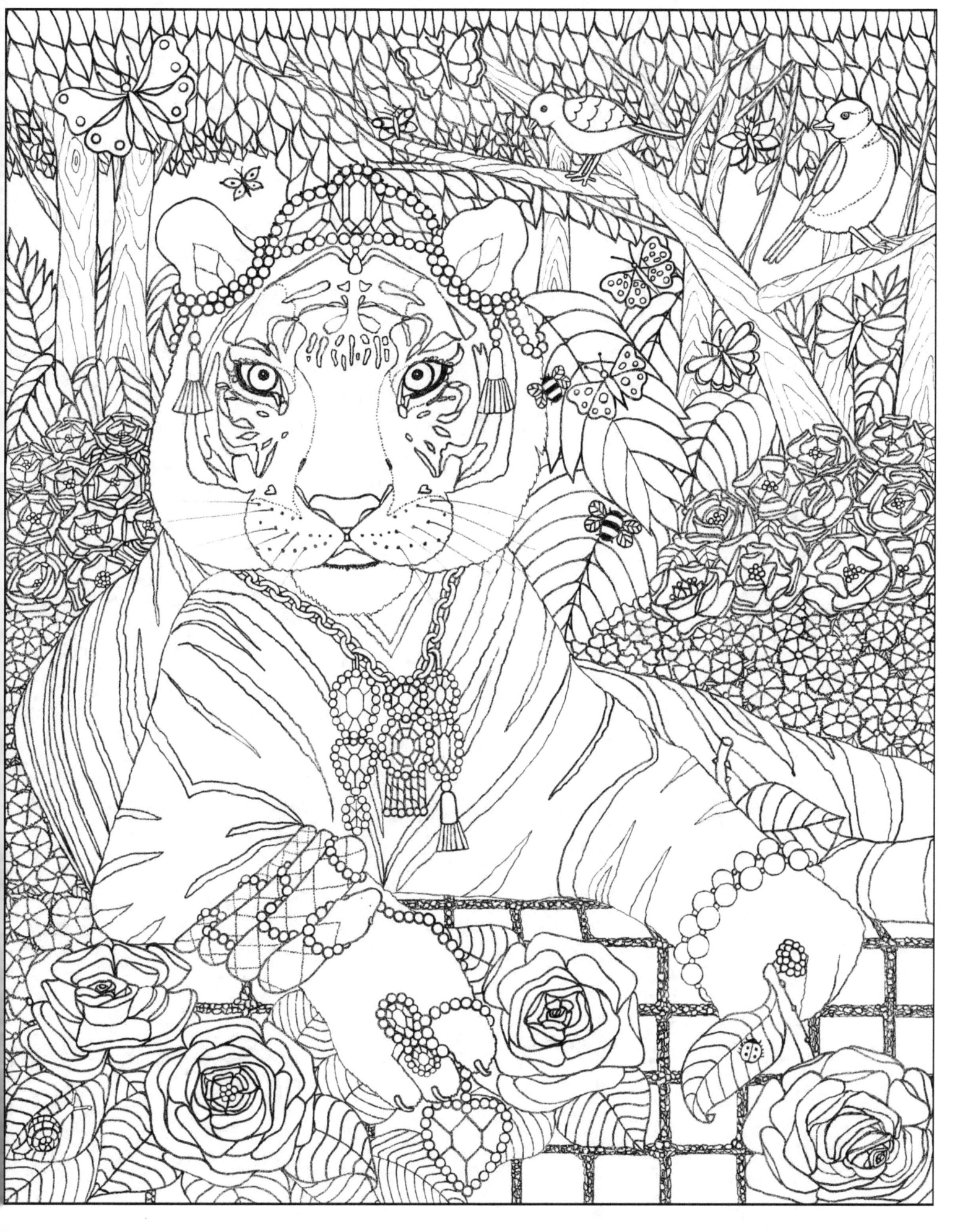

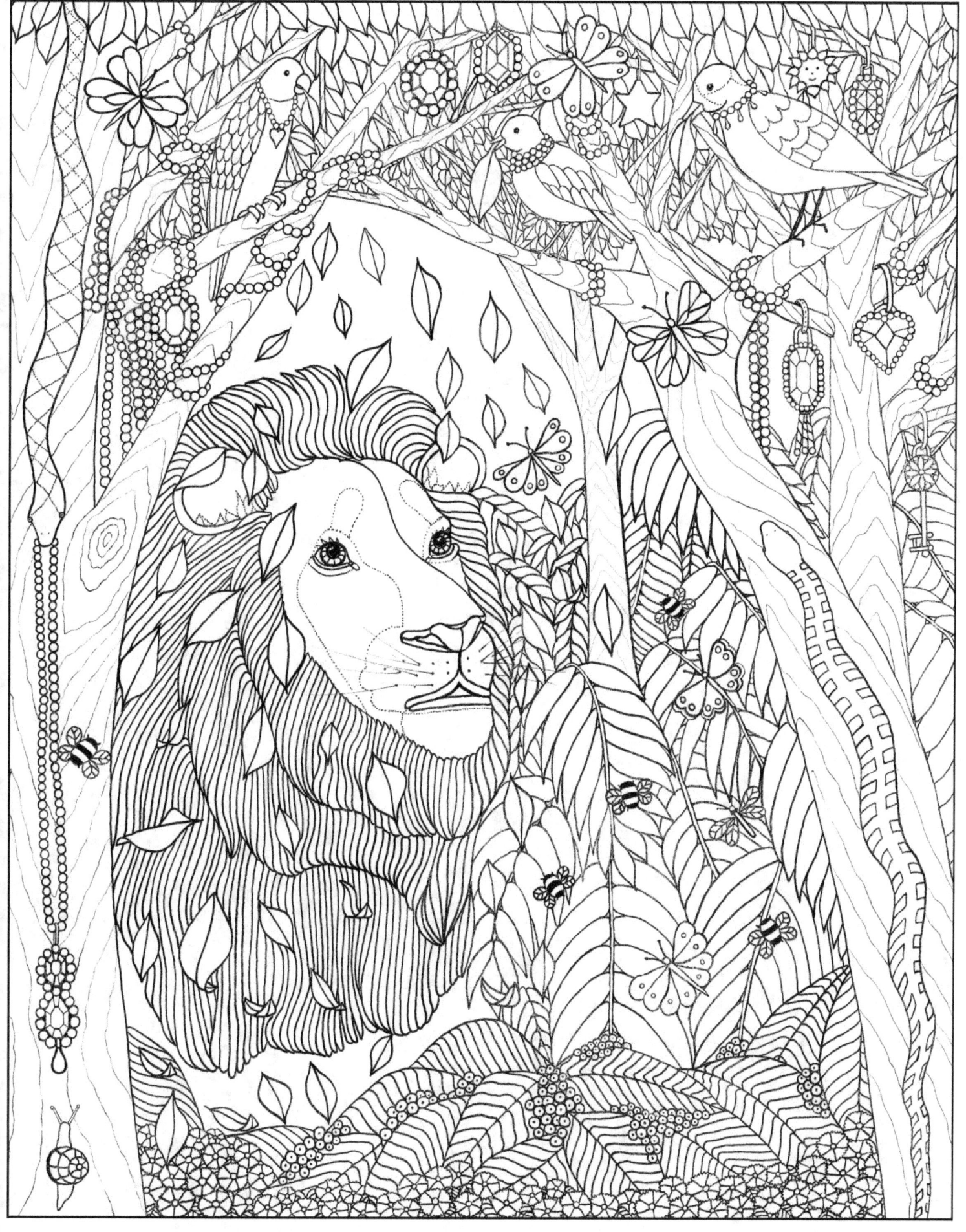

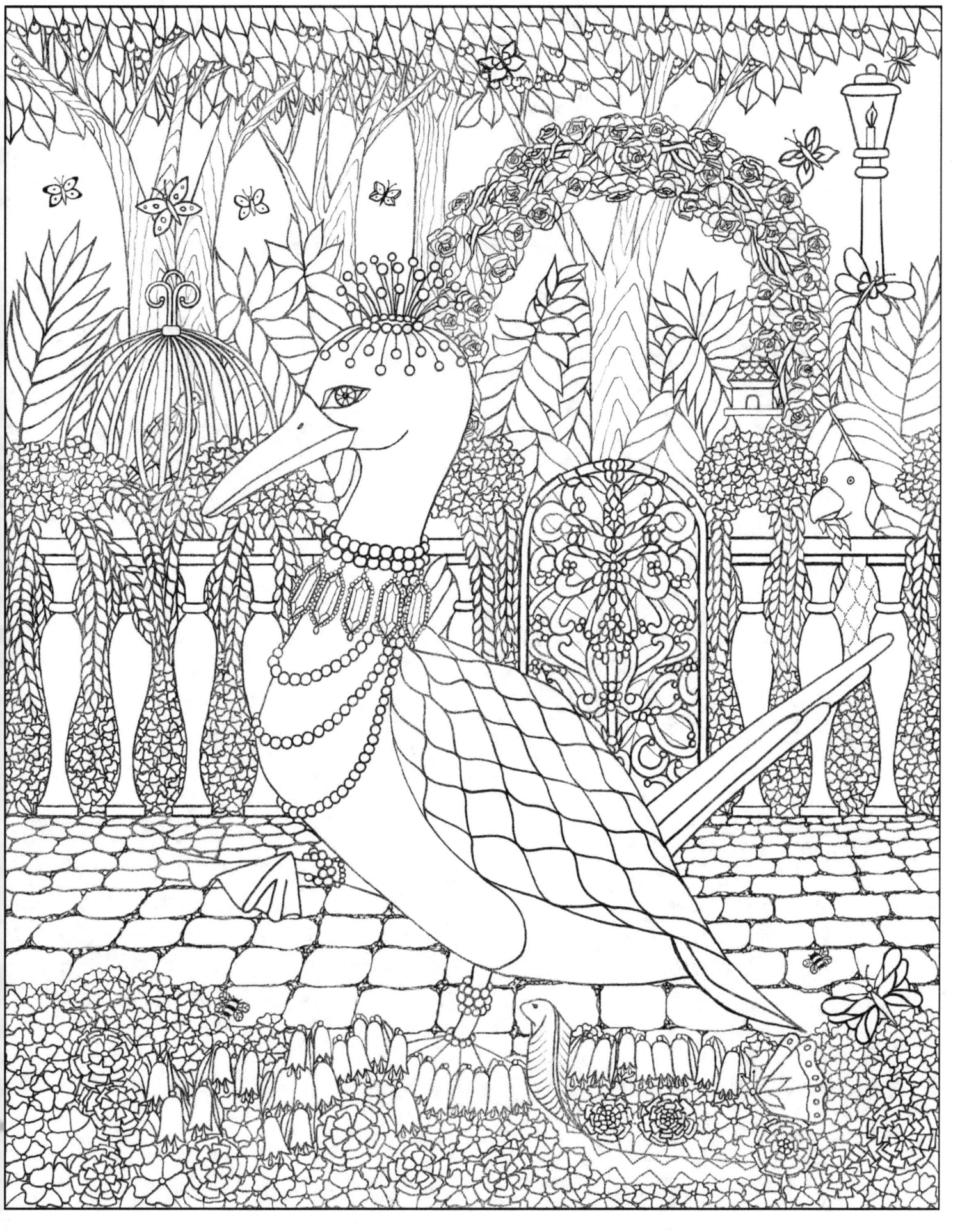

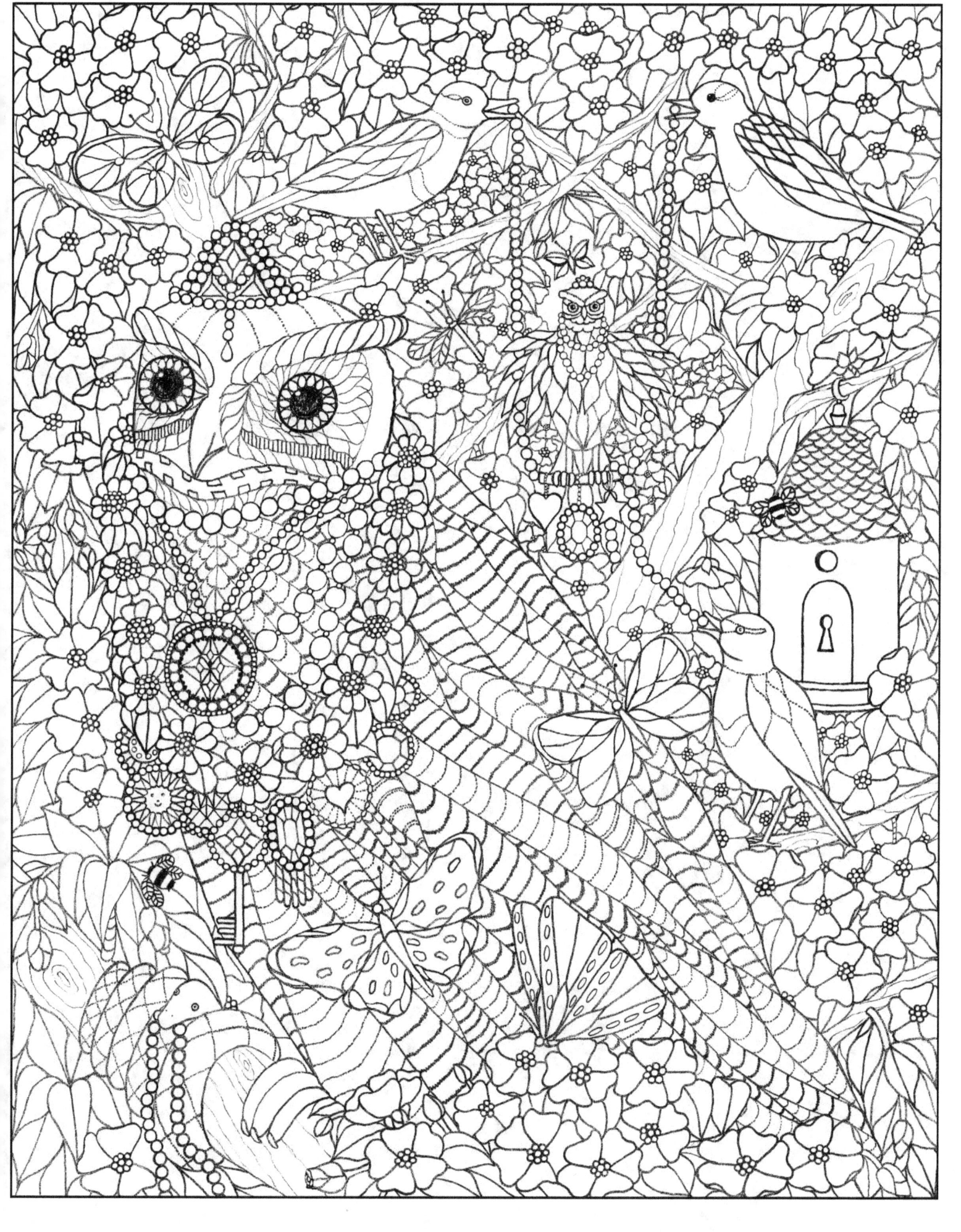

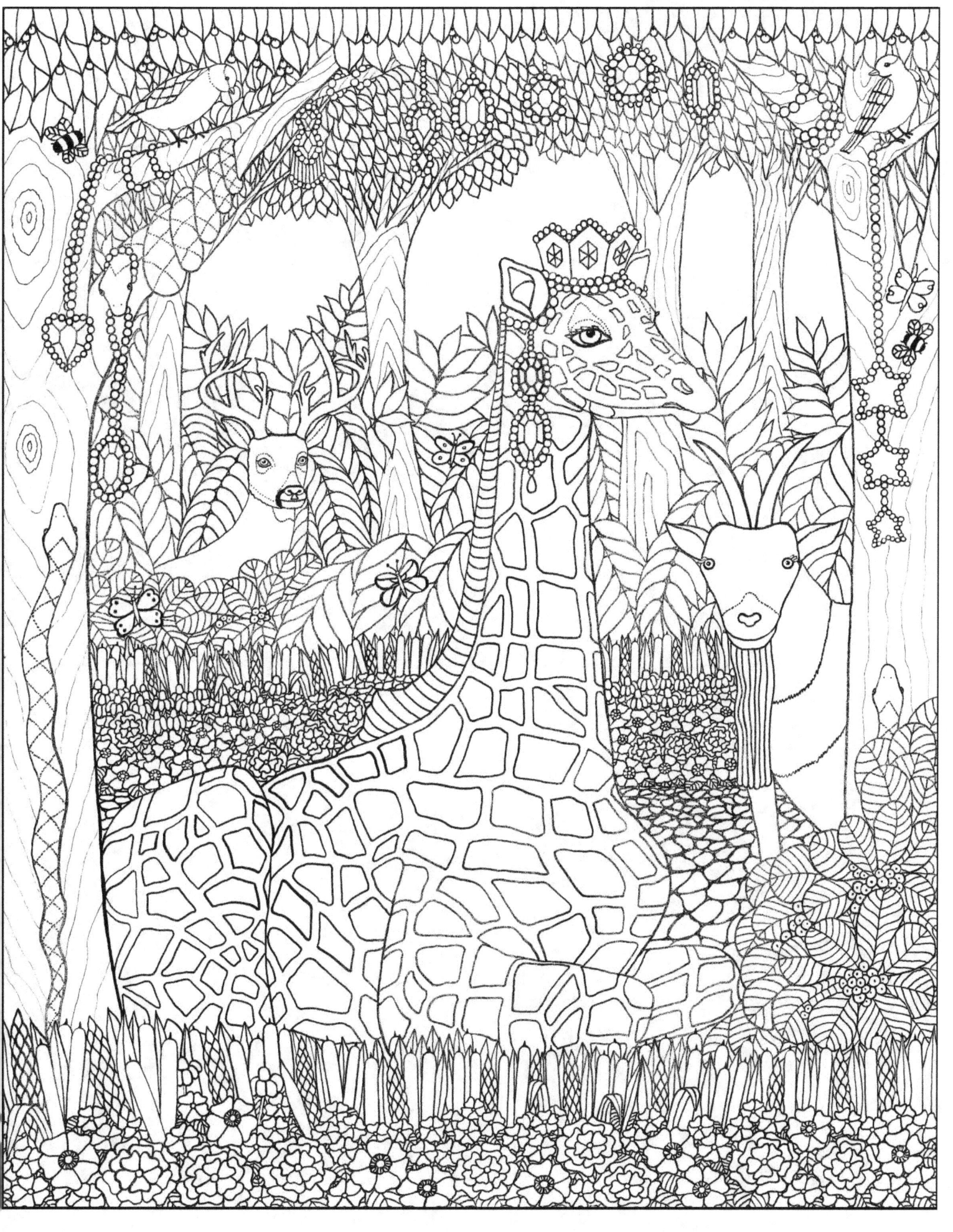

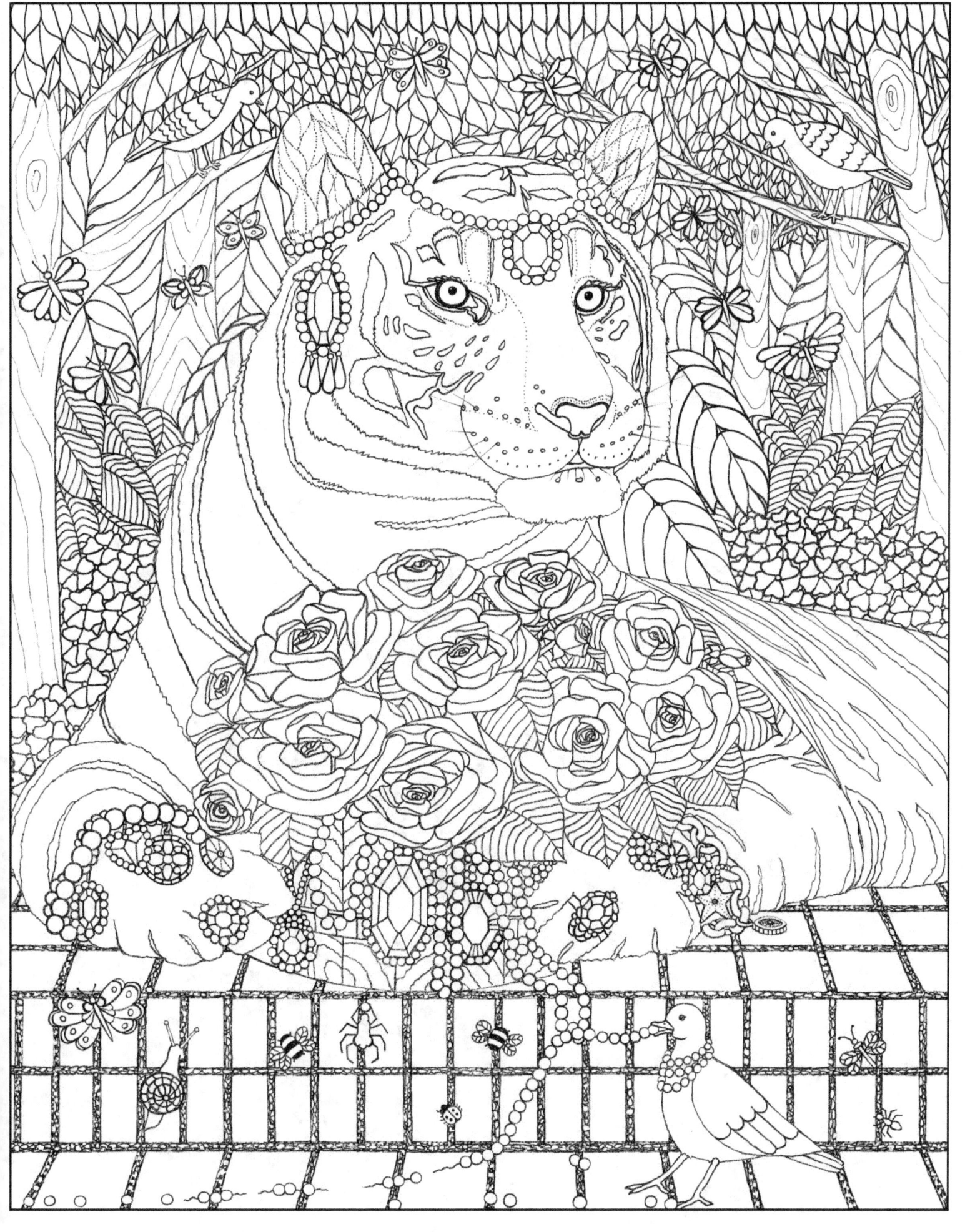

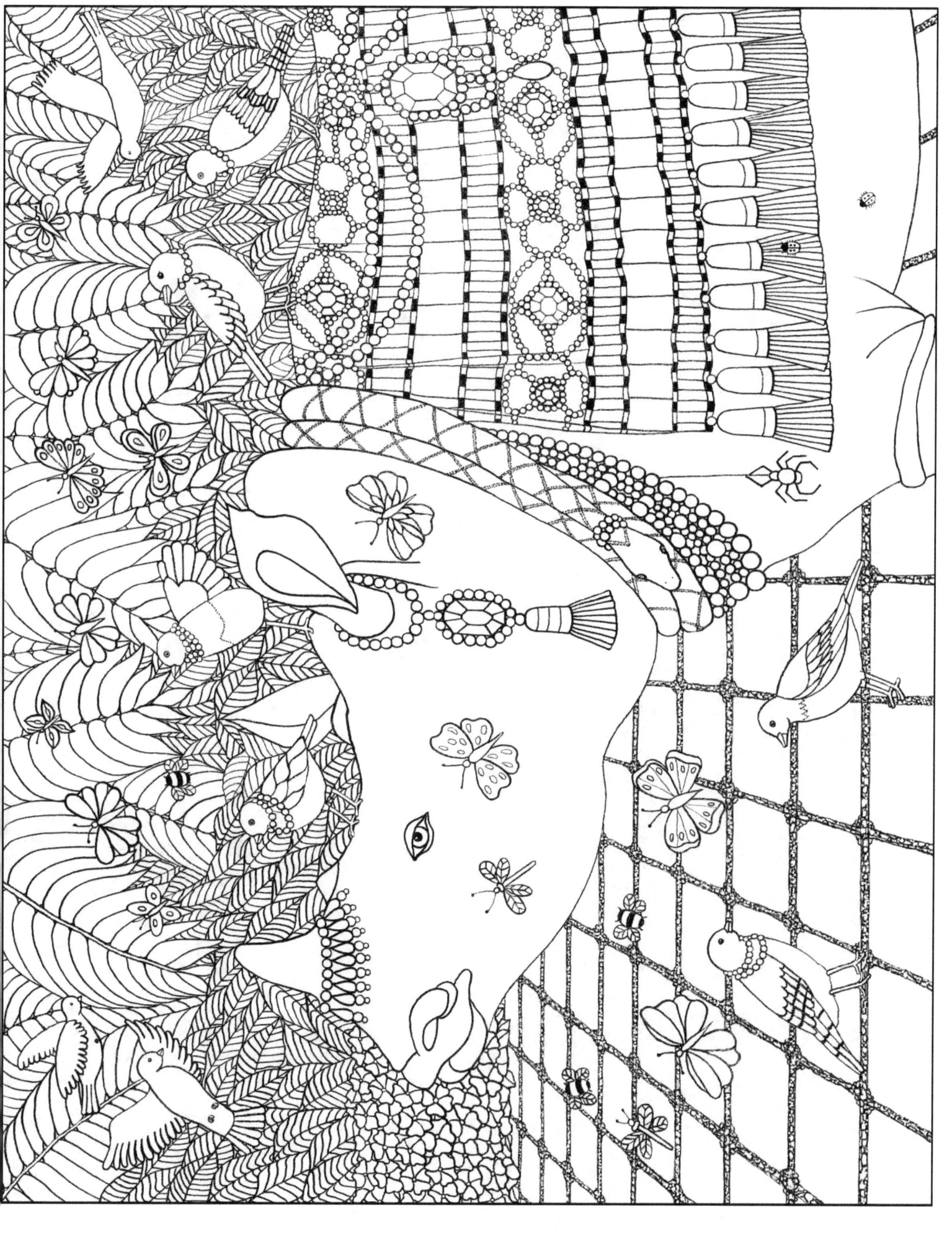

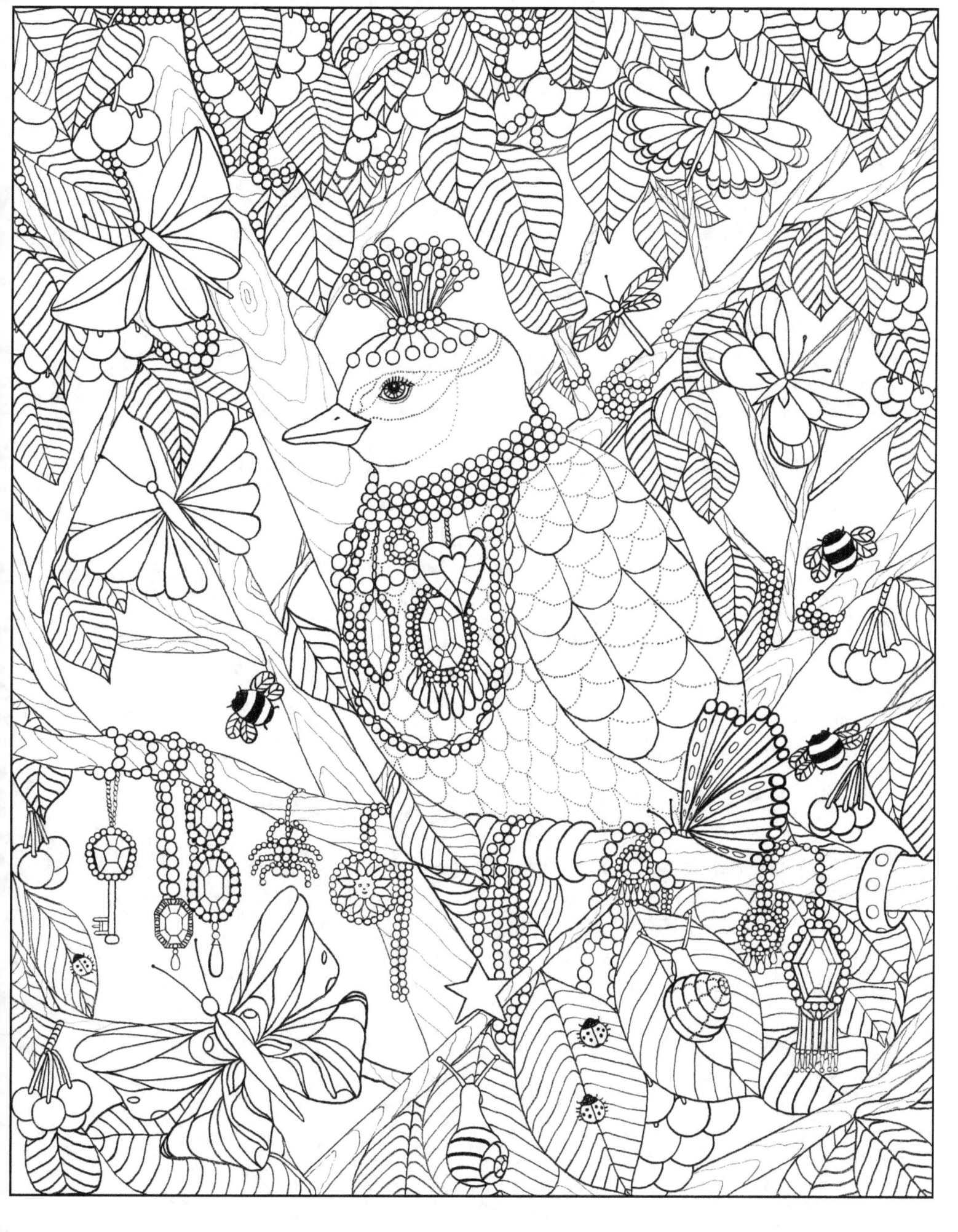

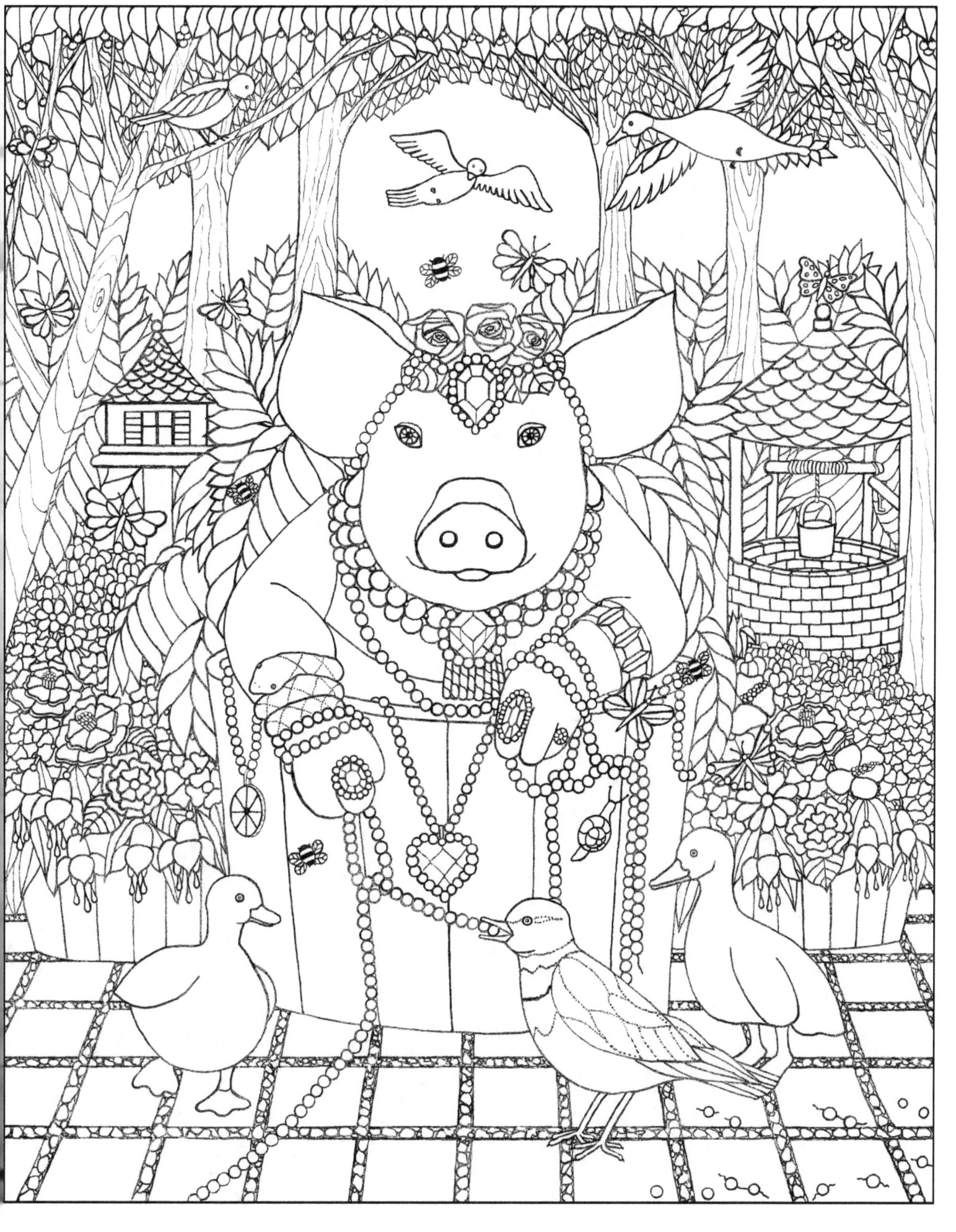

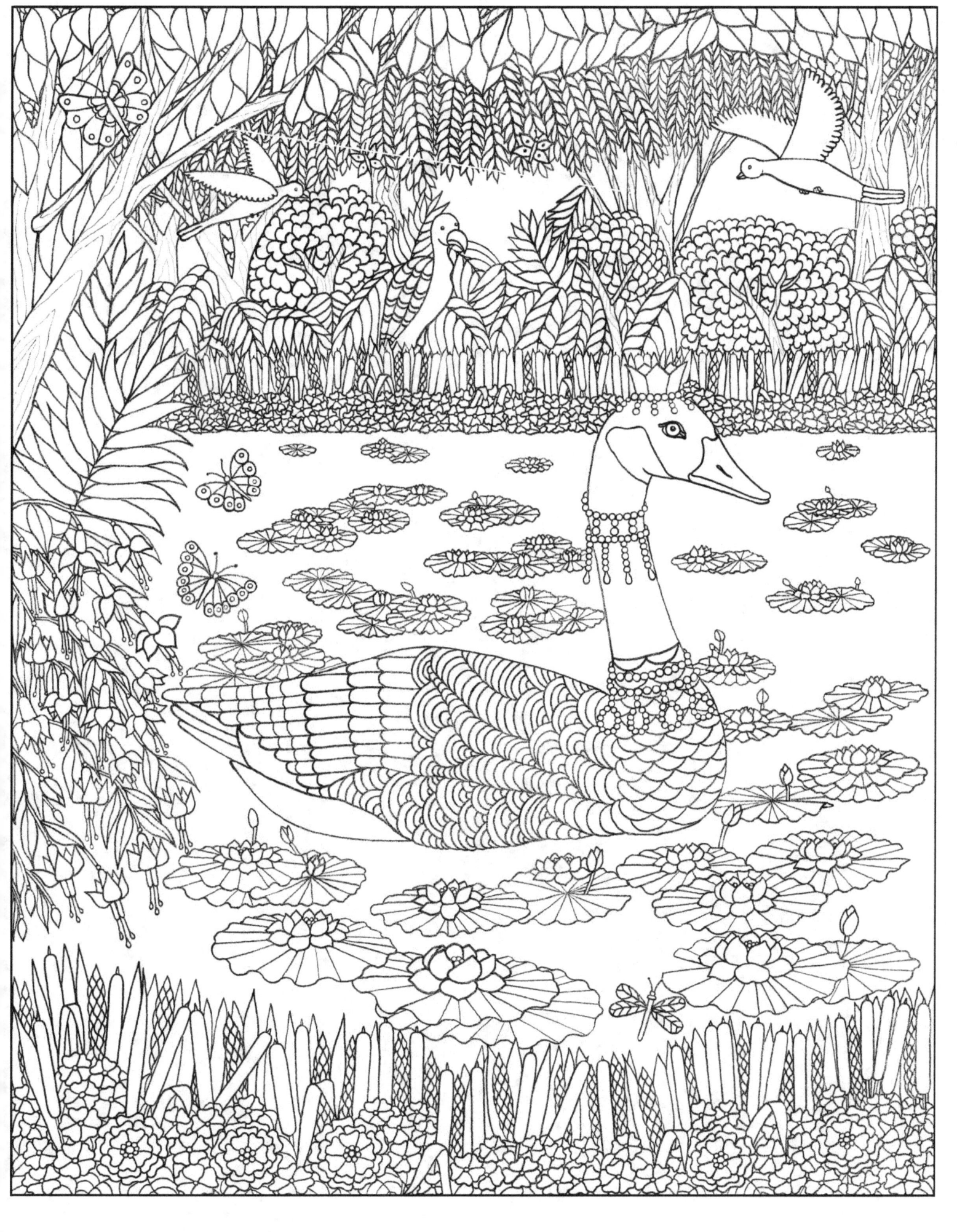

Beauty Area

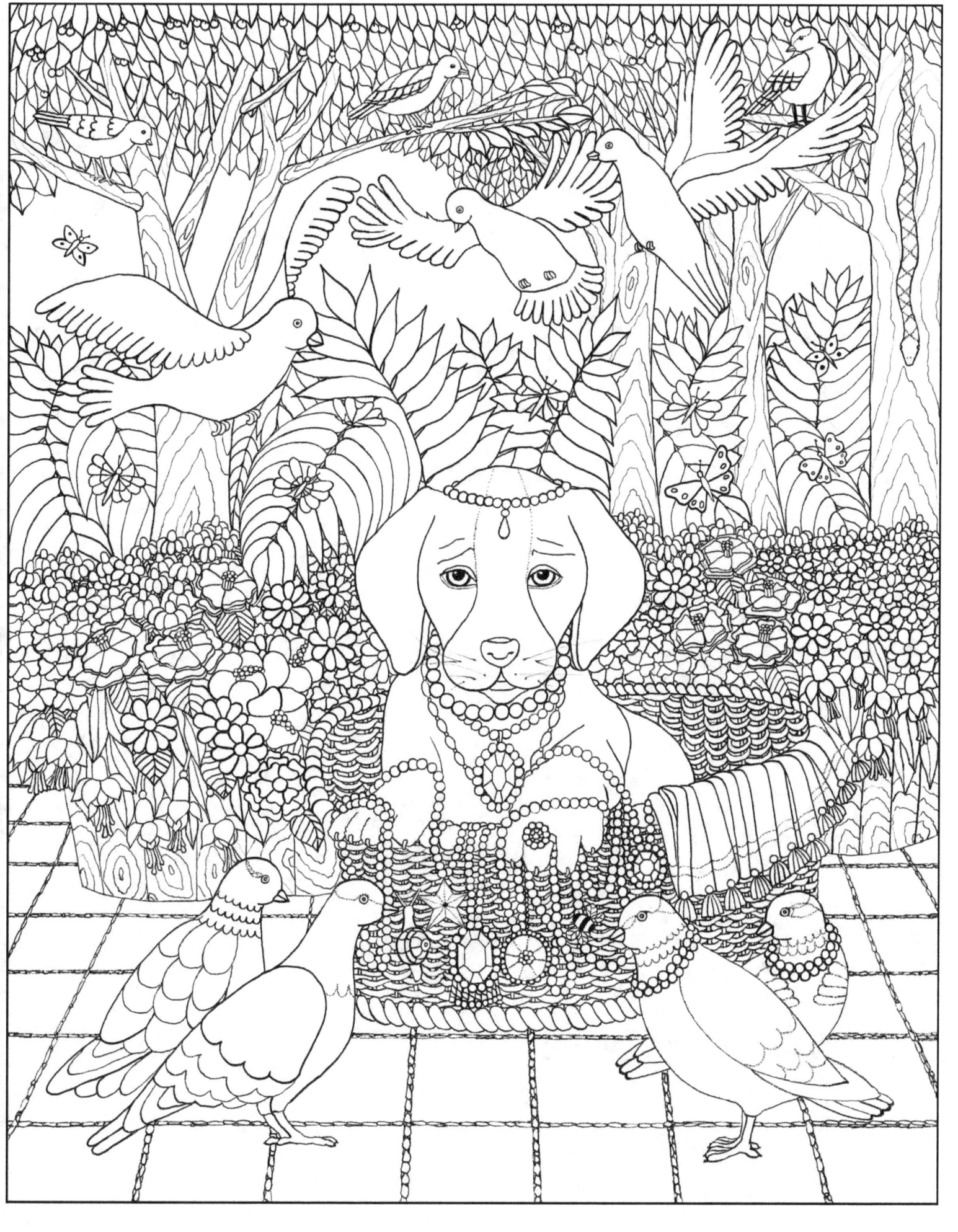

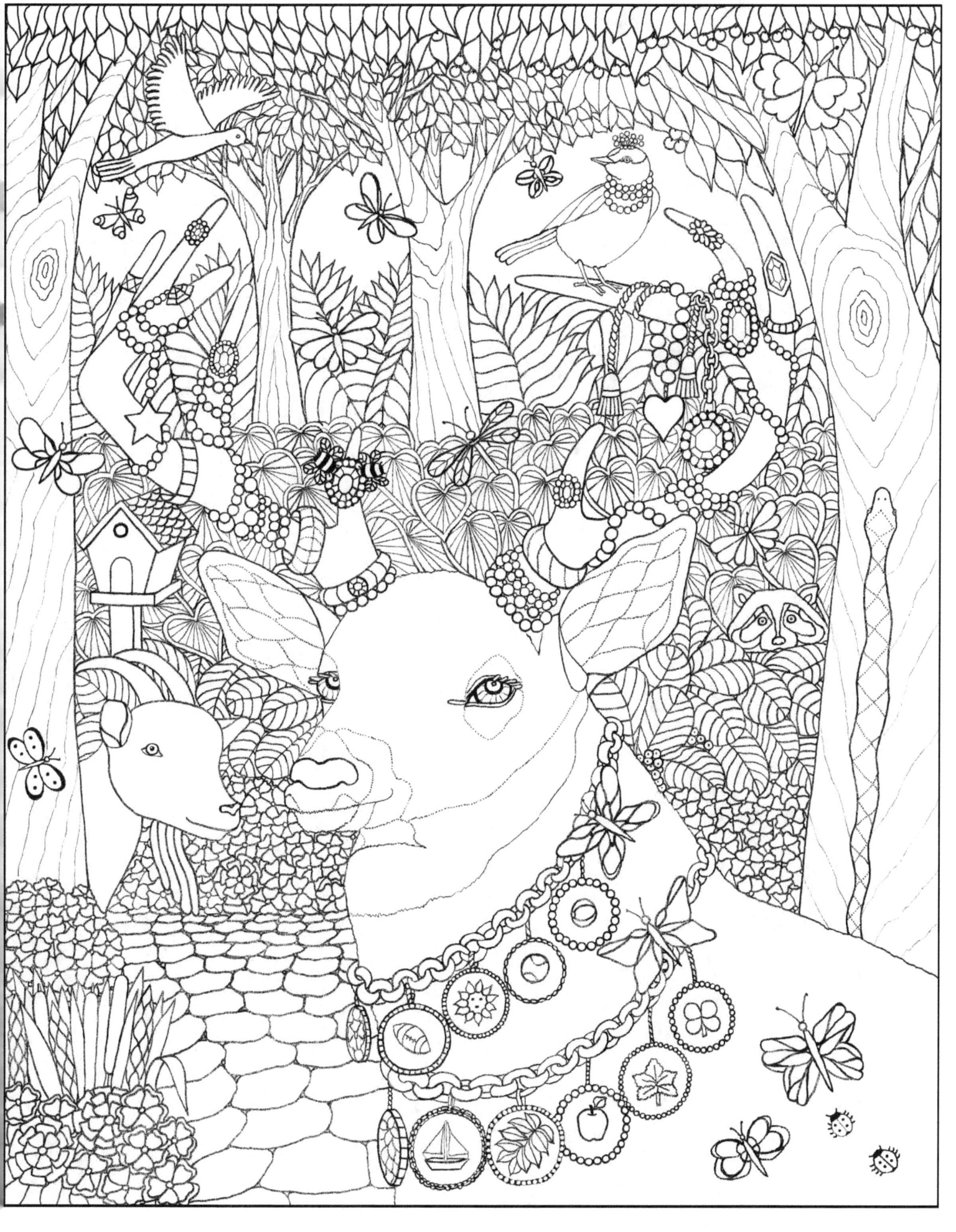

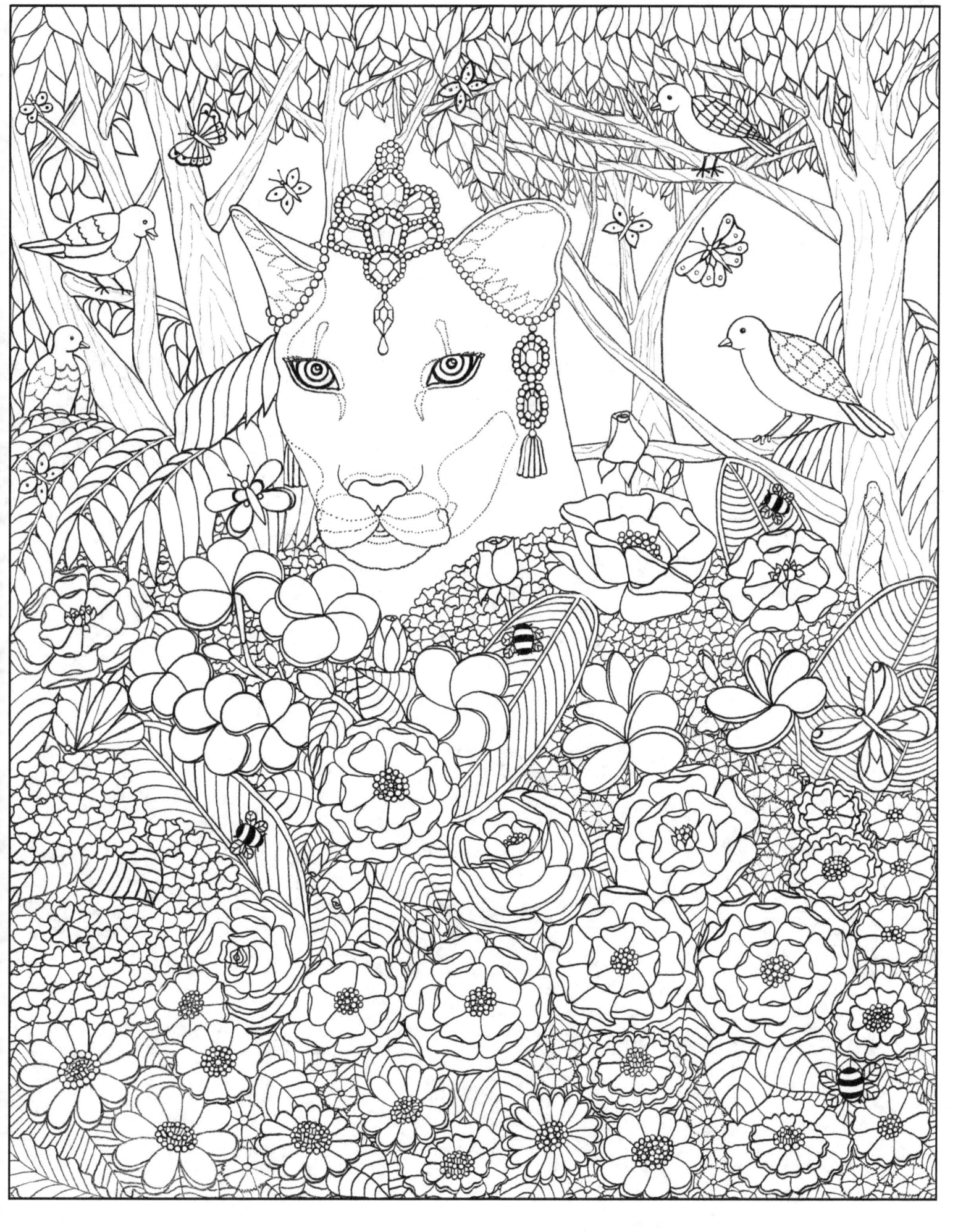

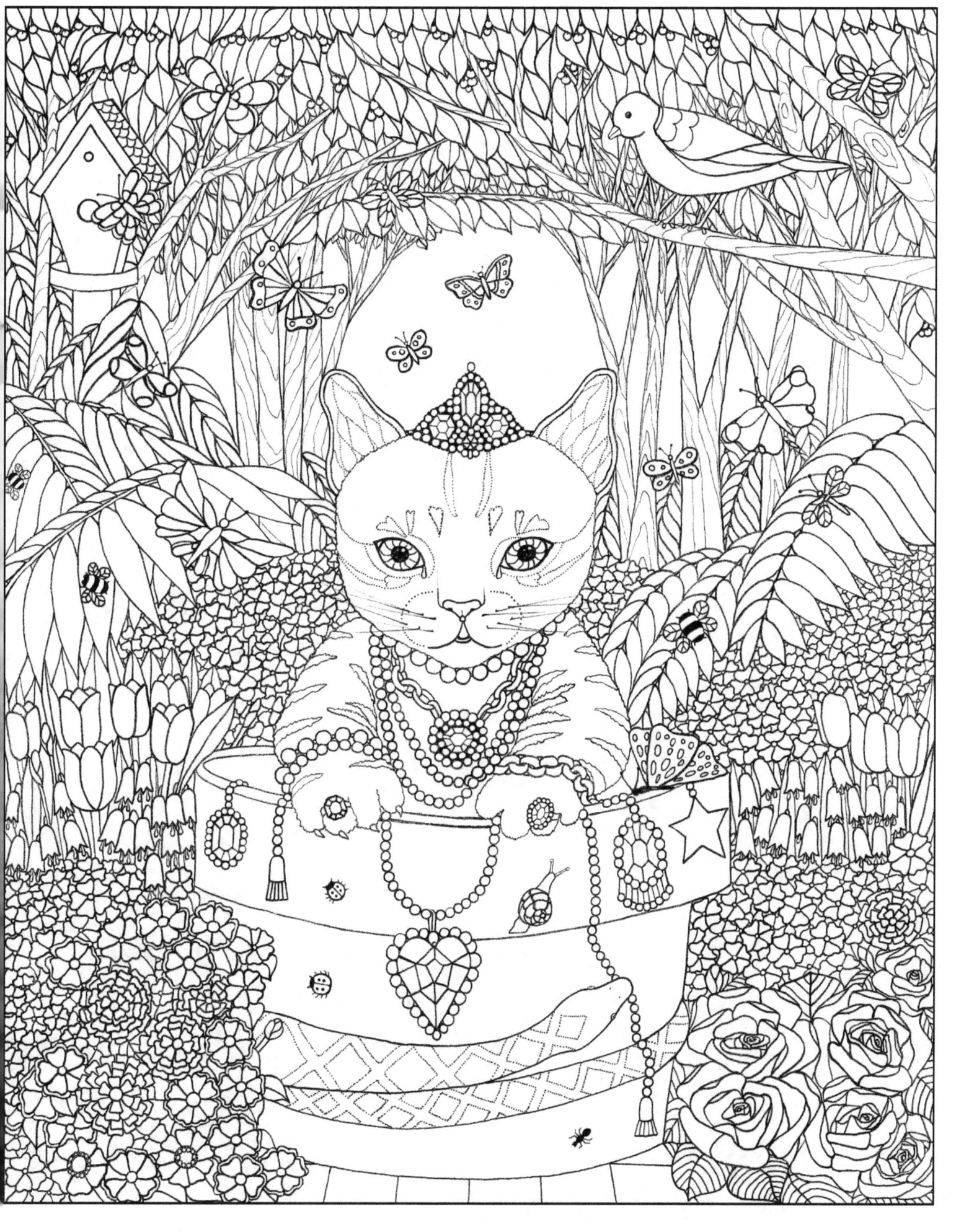

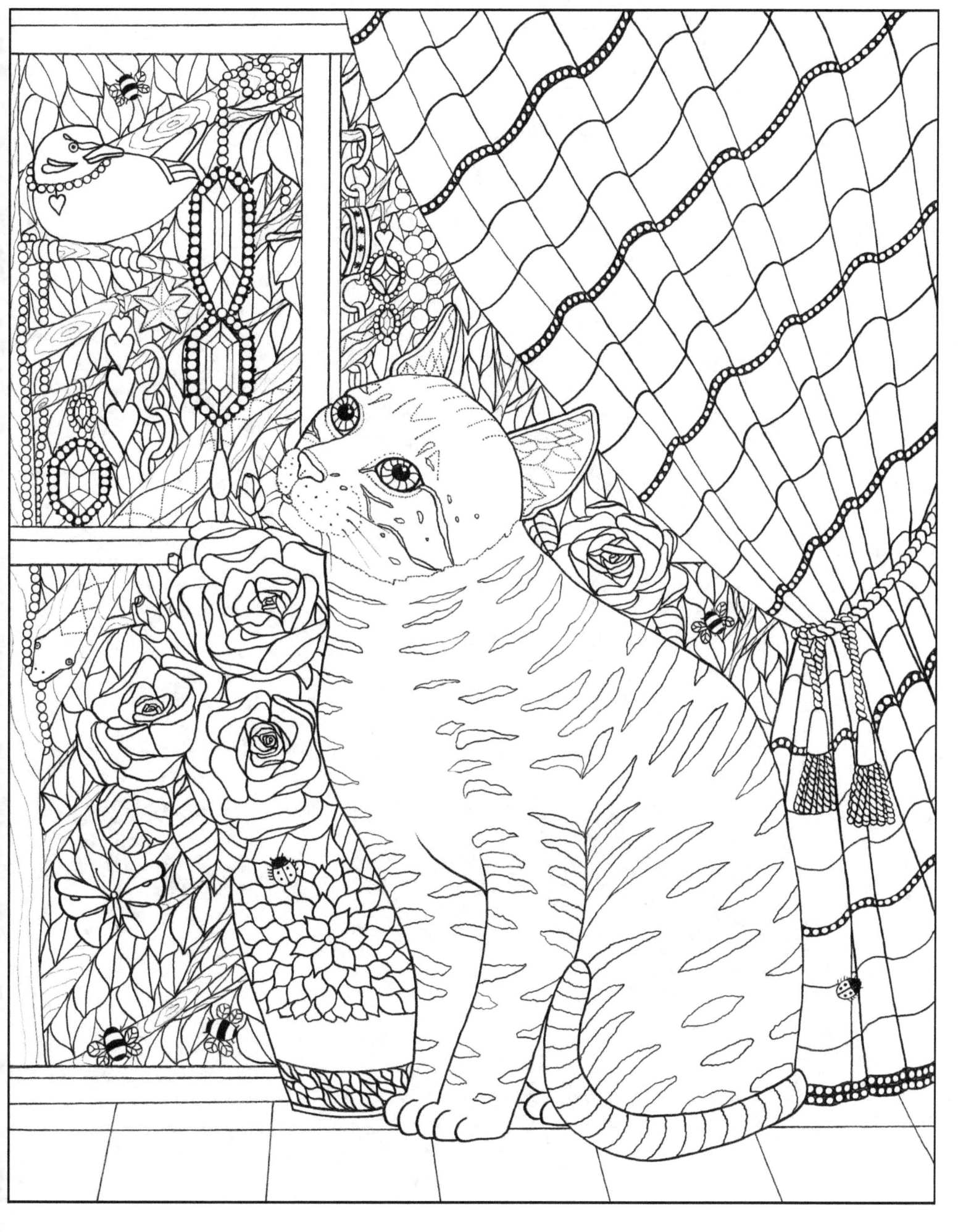

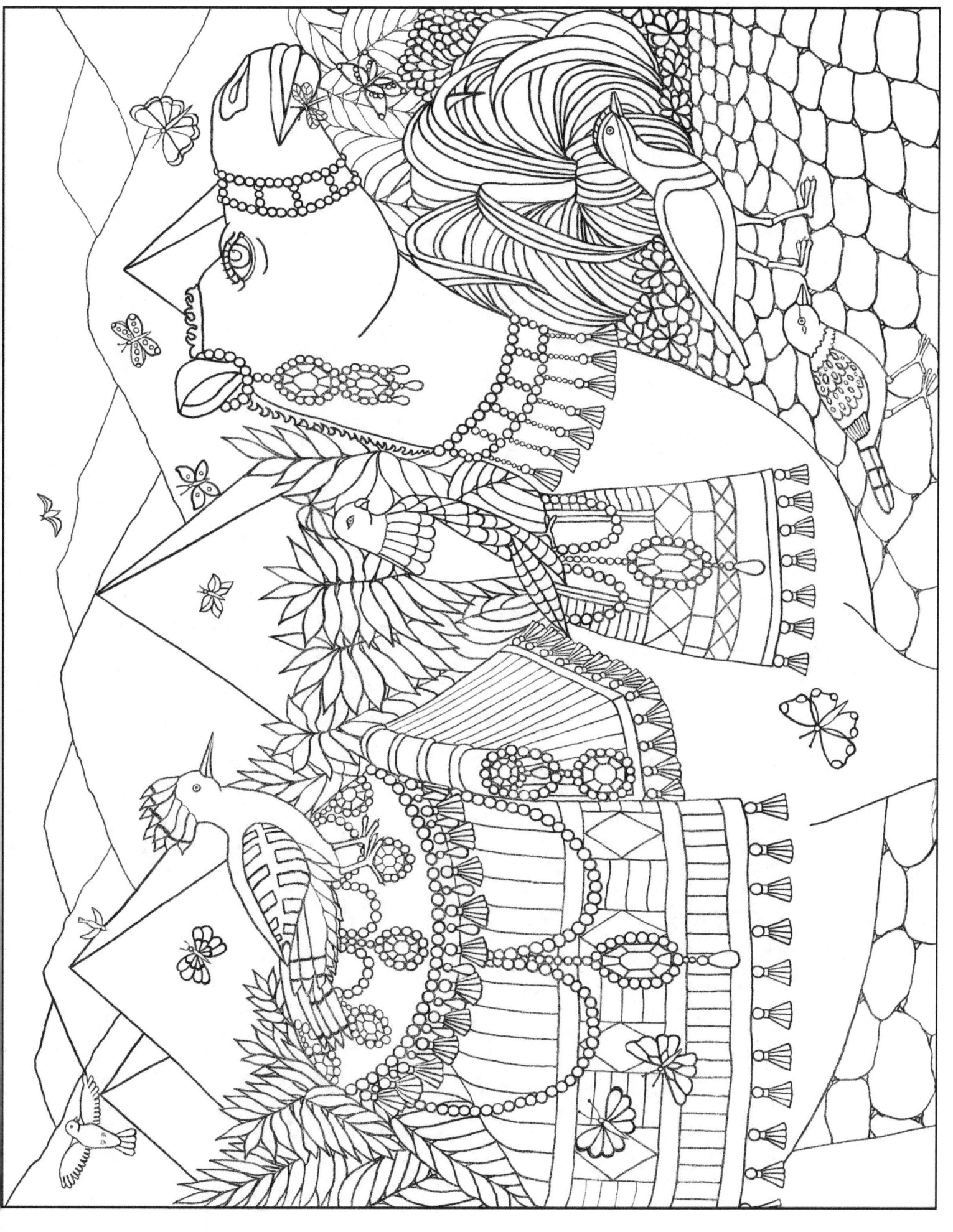

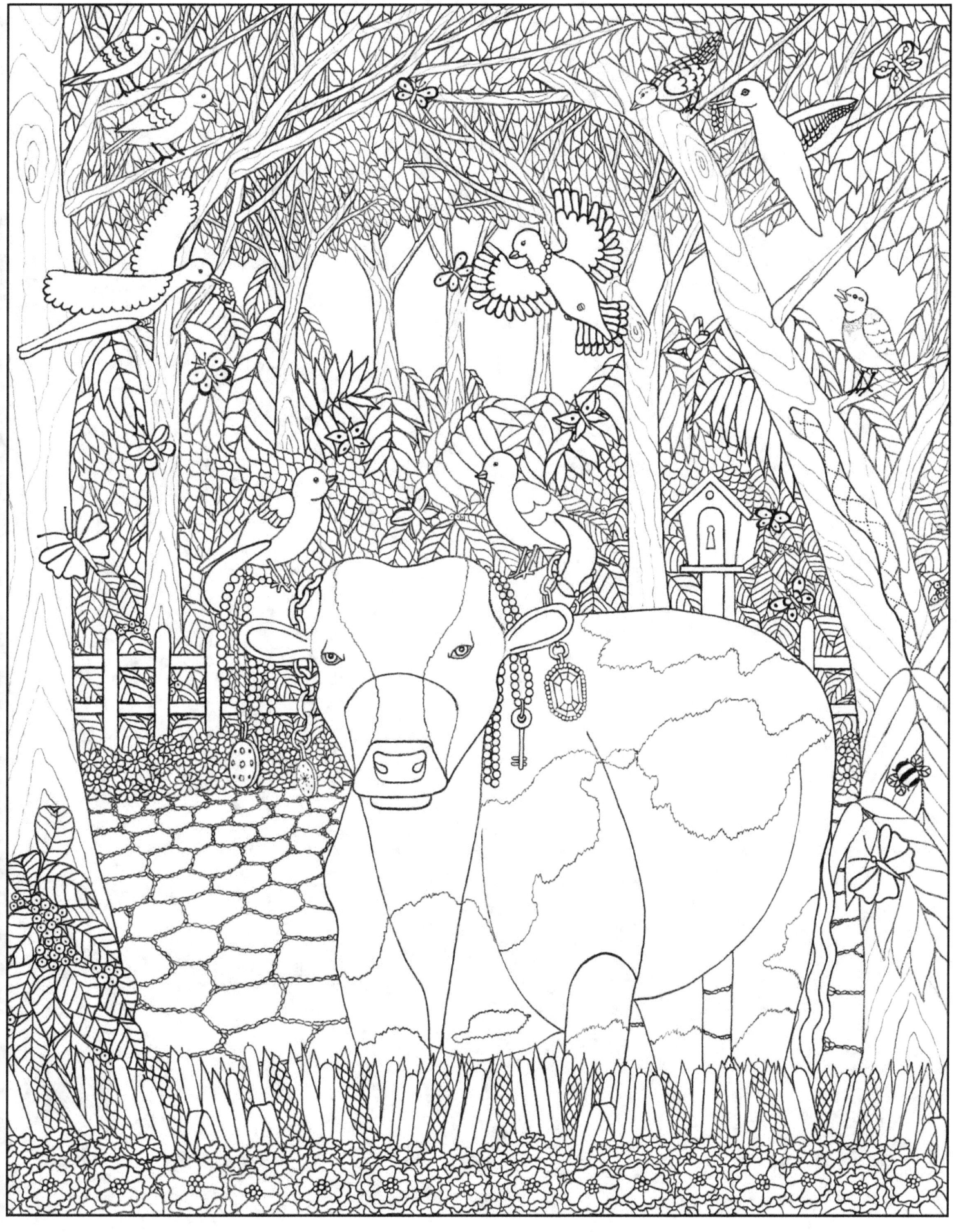

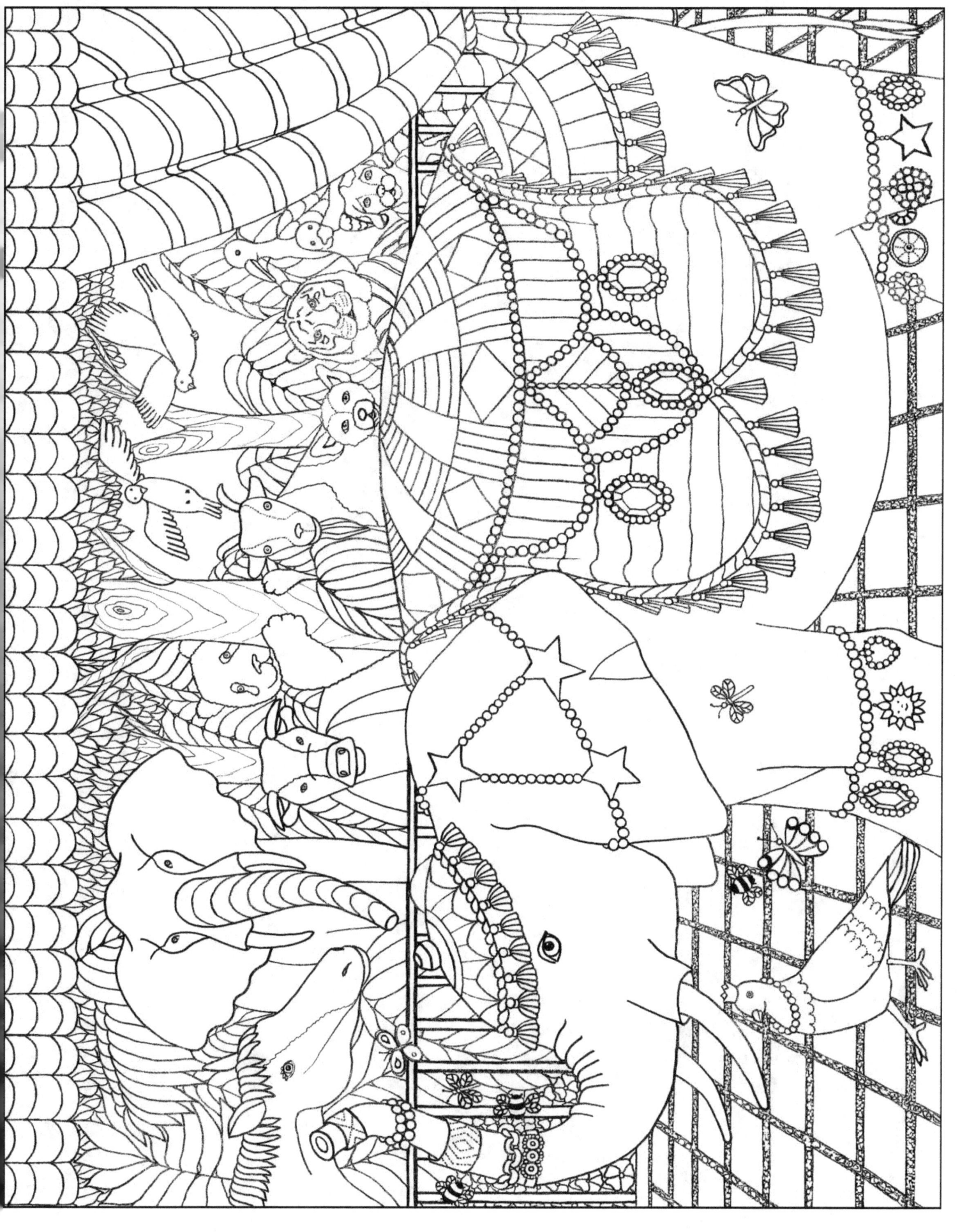

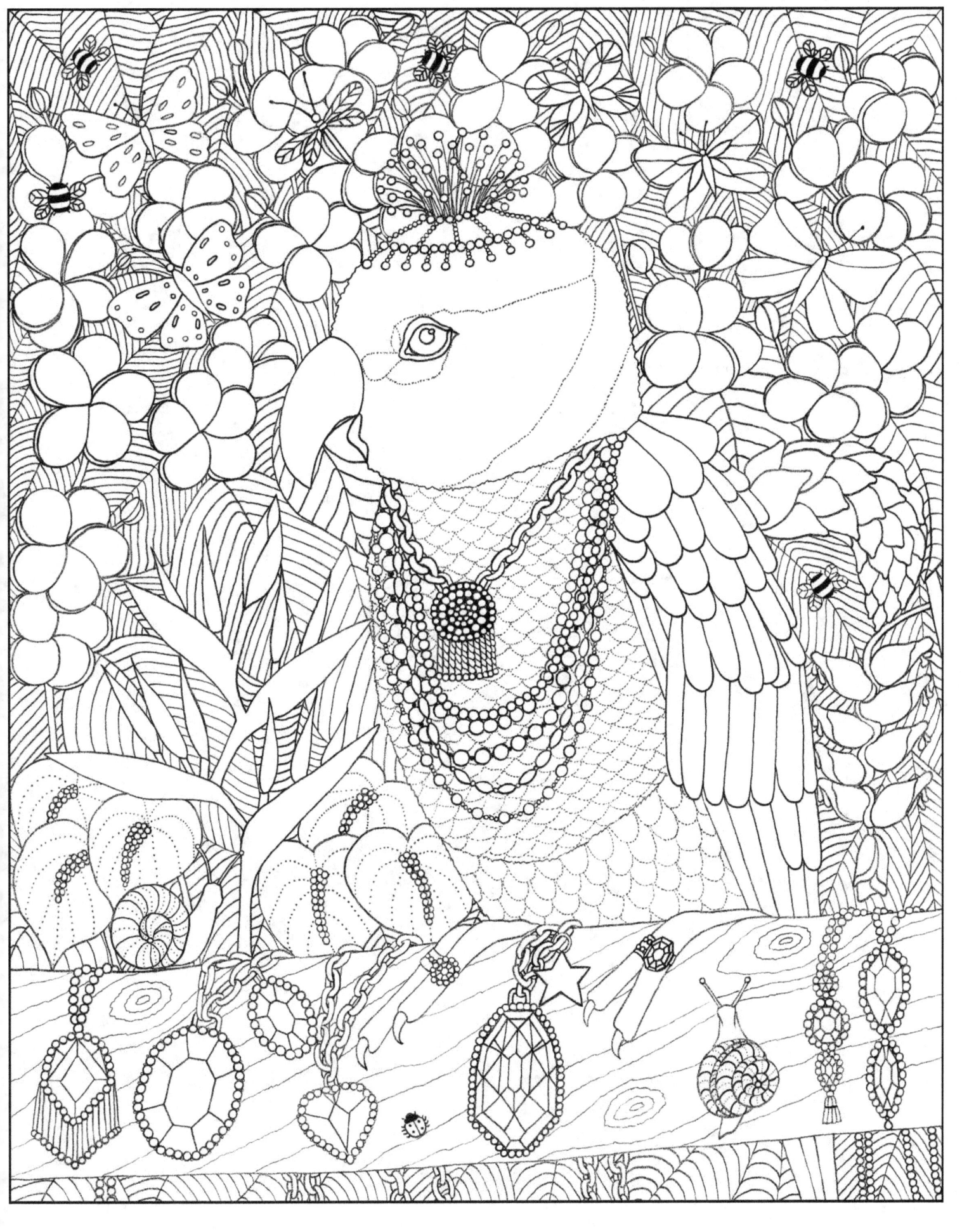

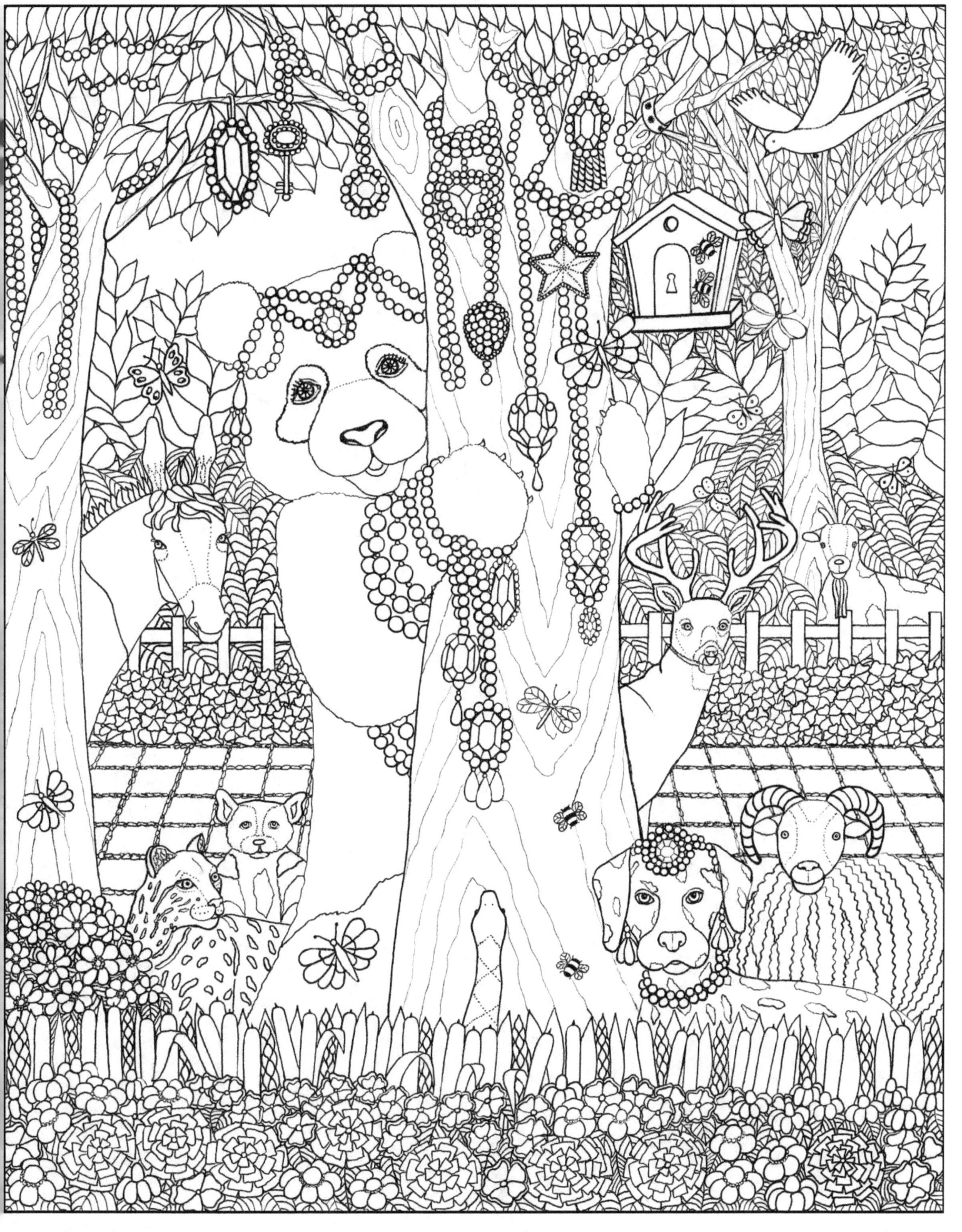

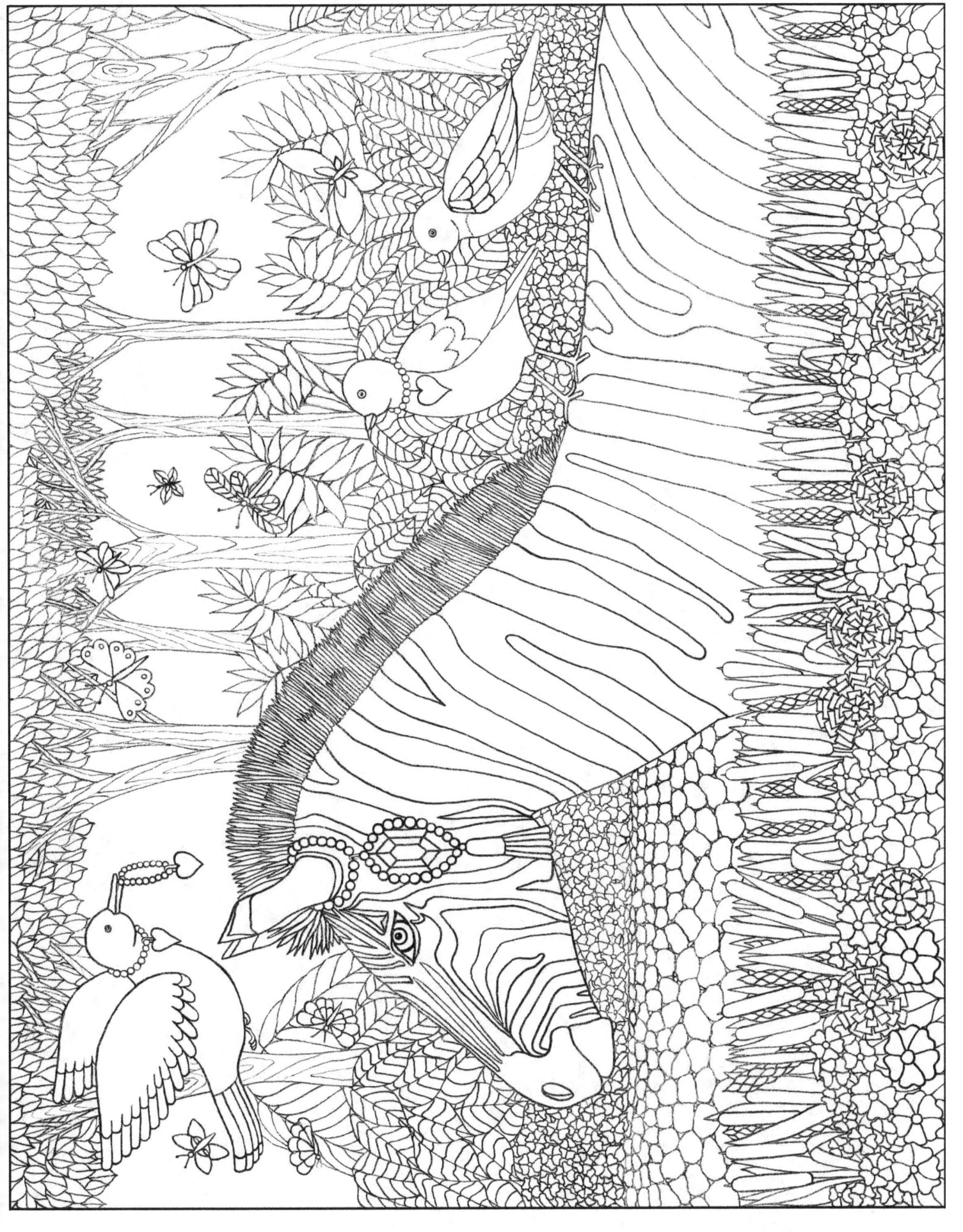

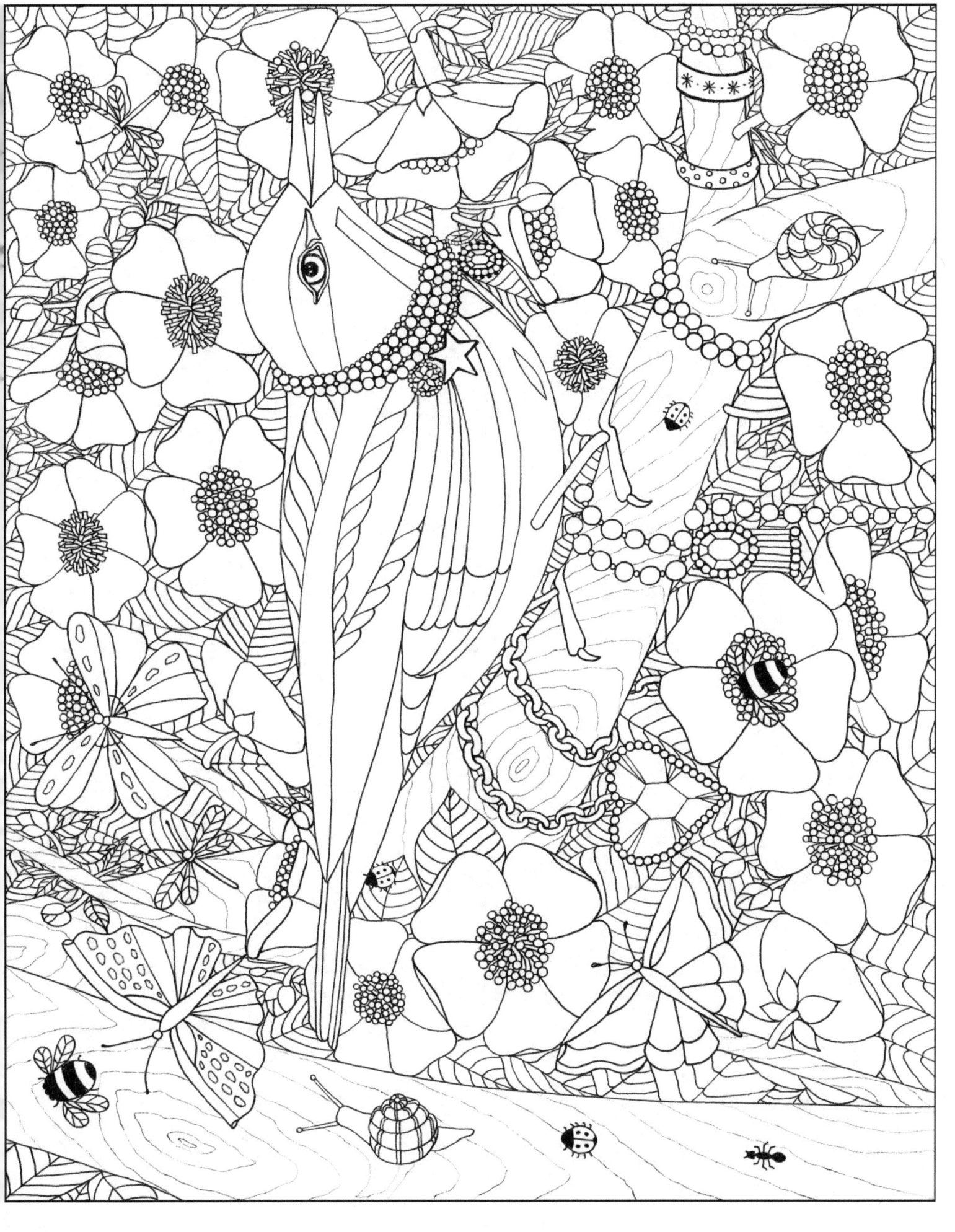

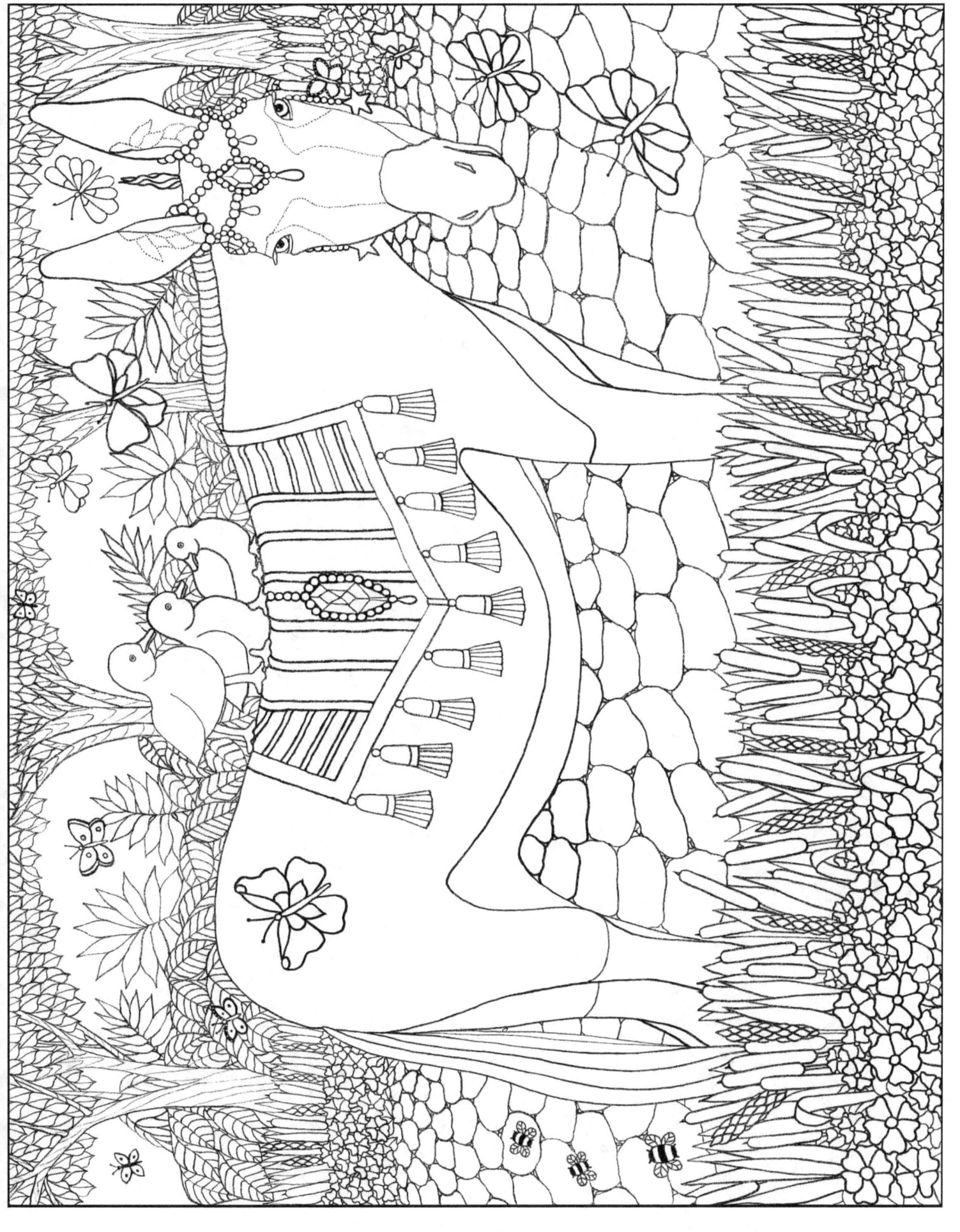

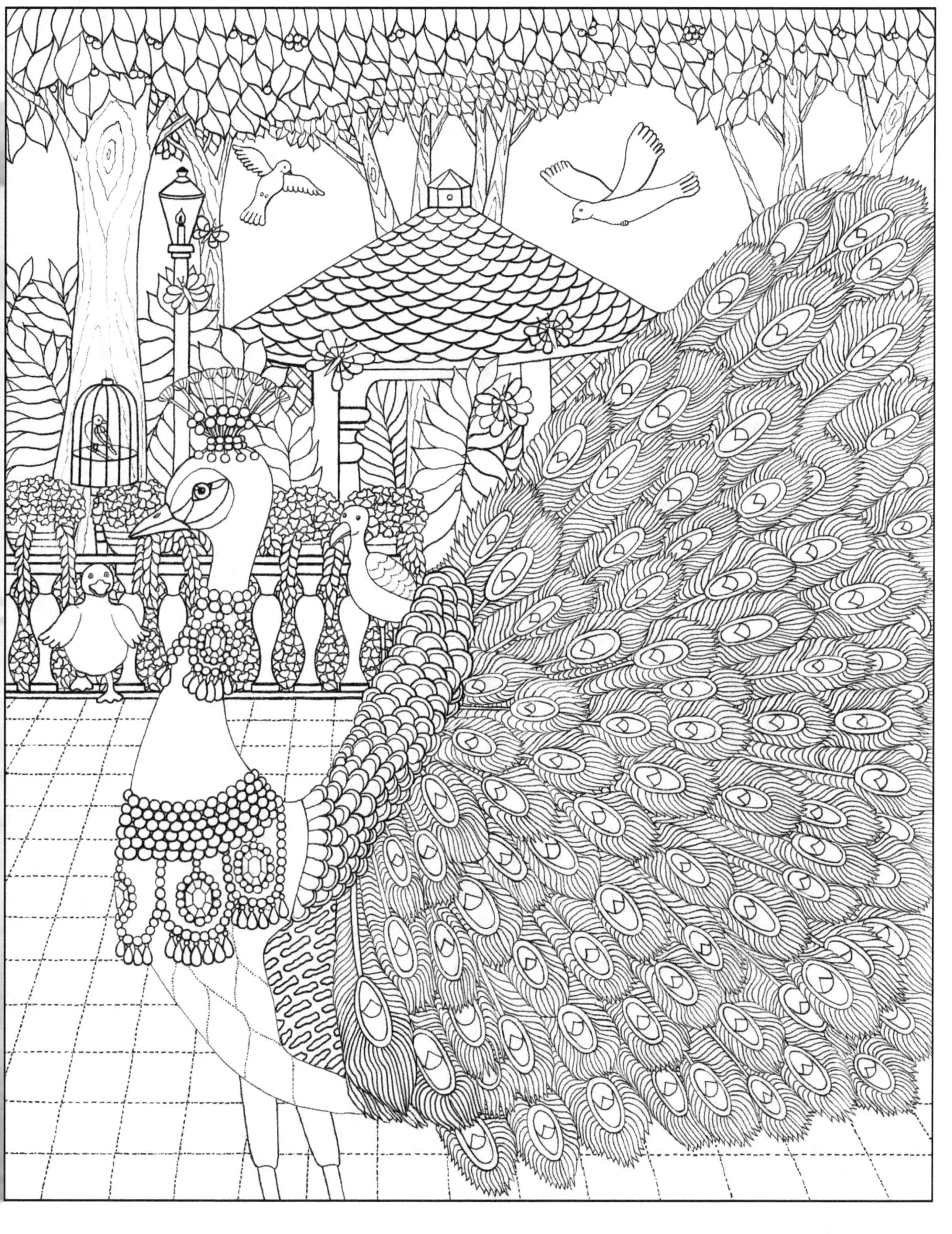

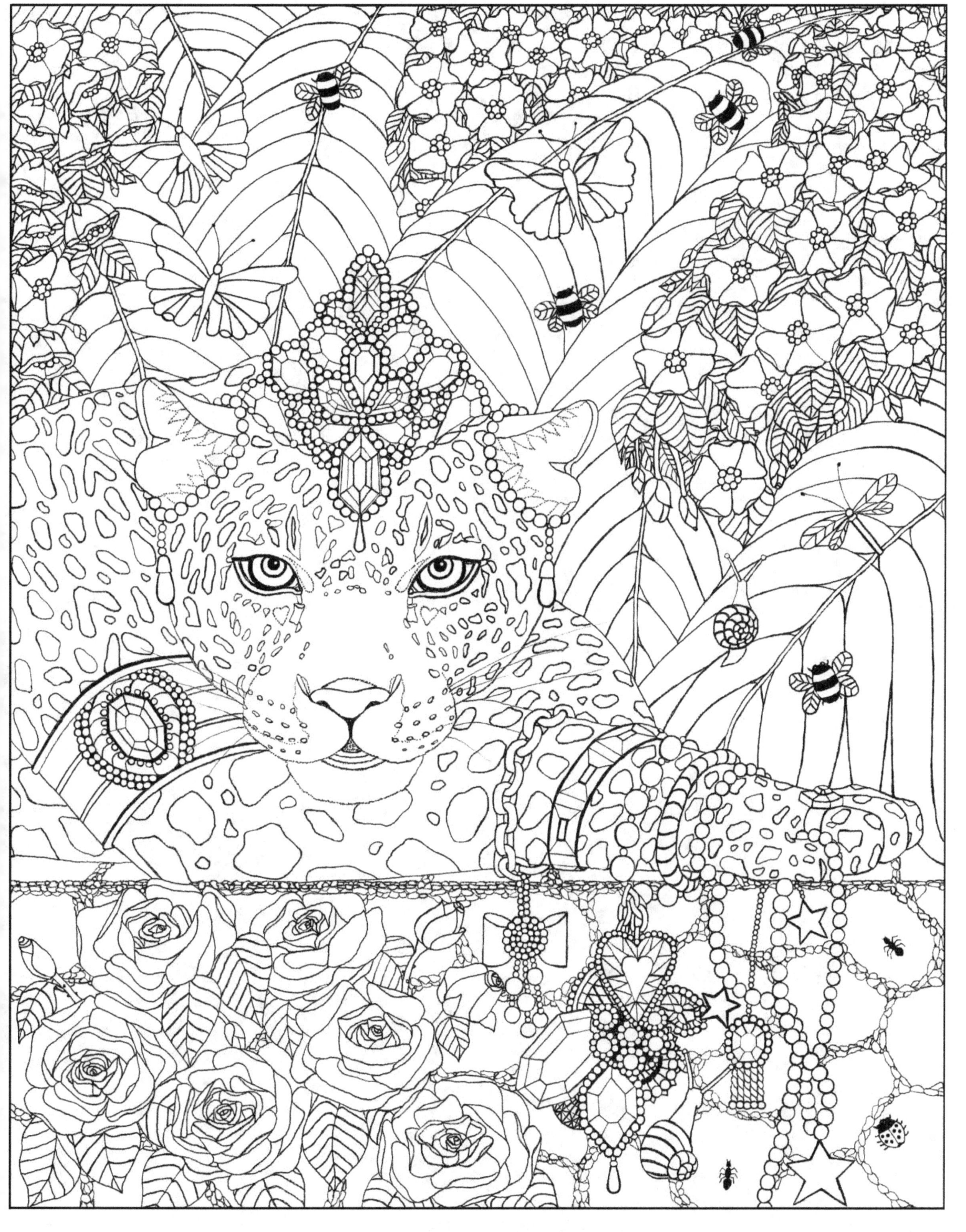

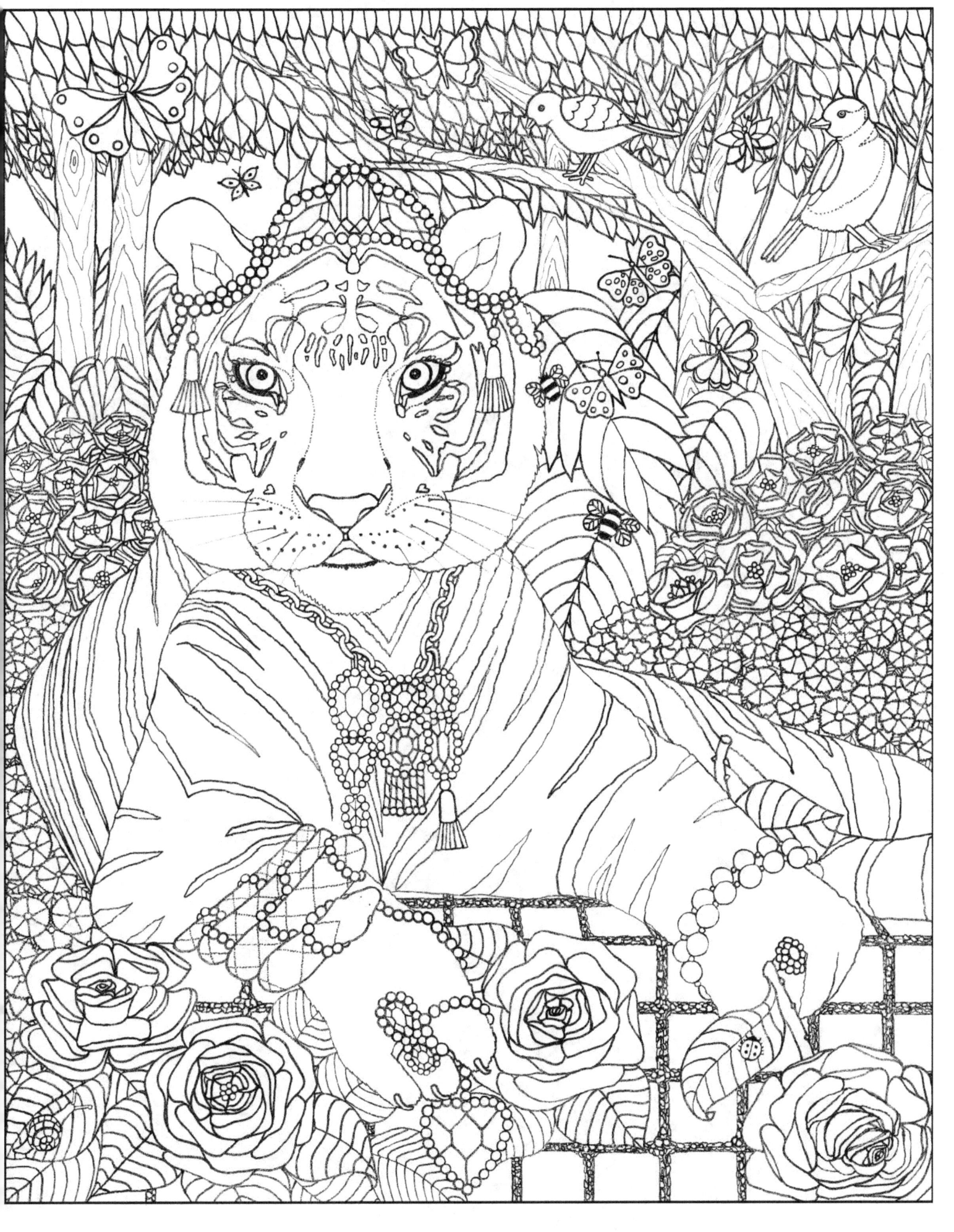

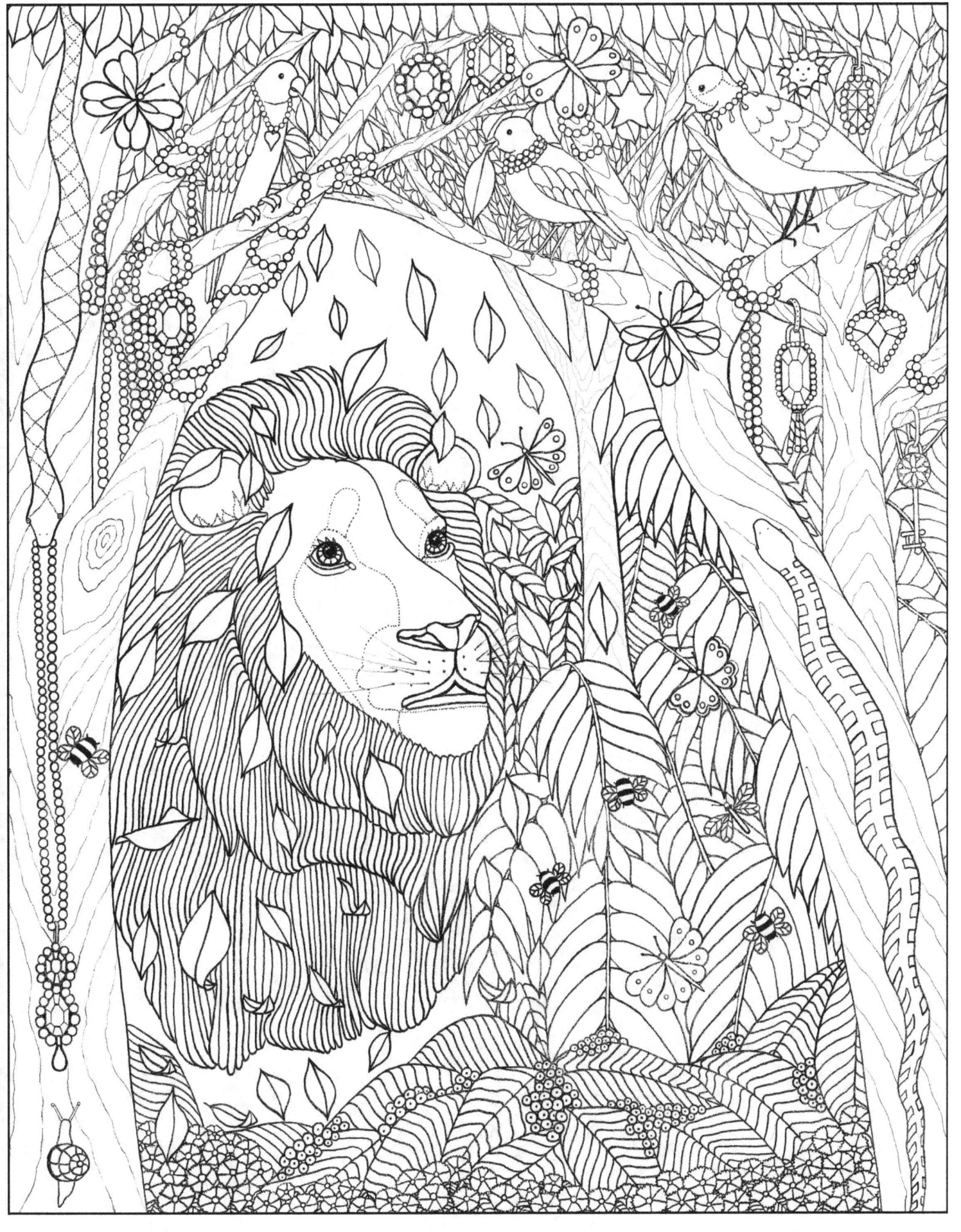

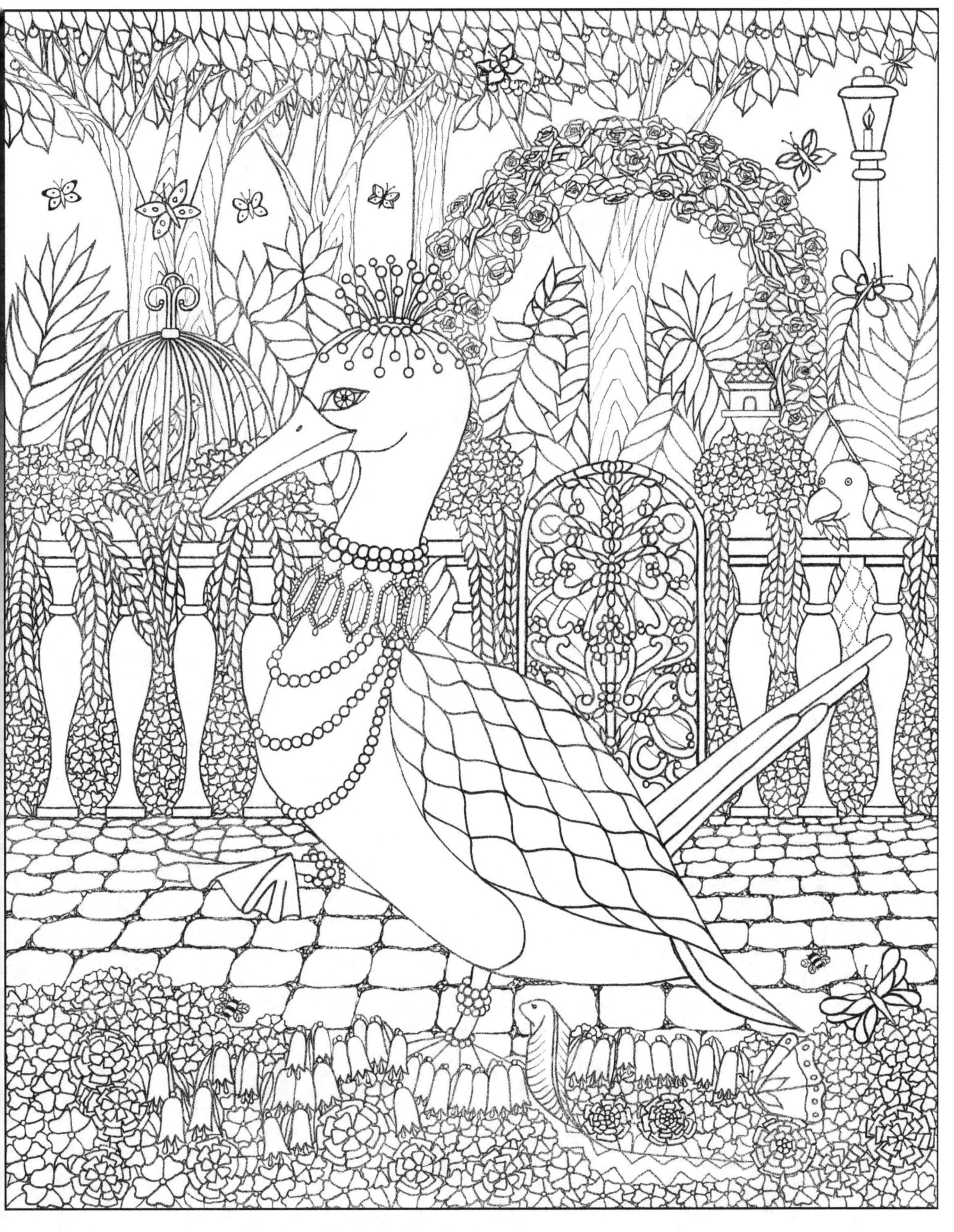

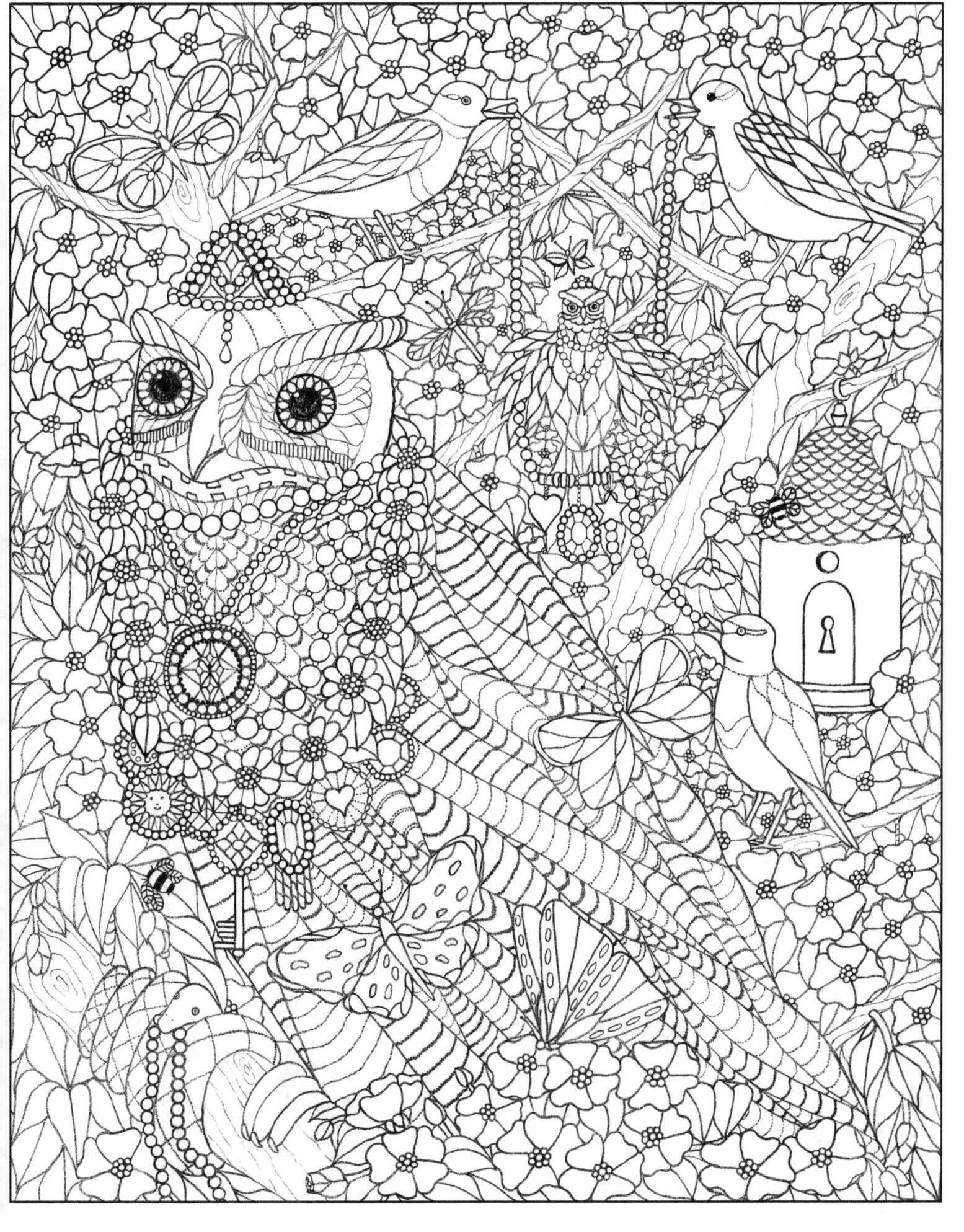

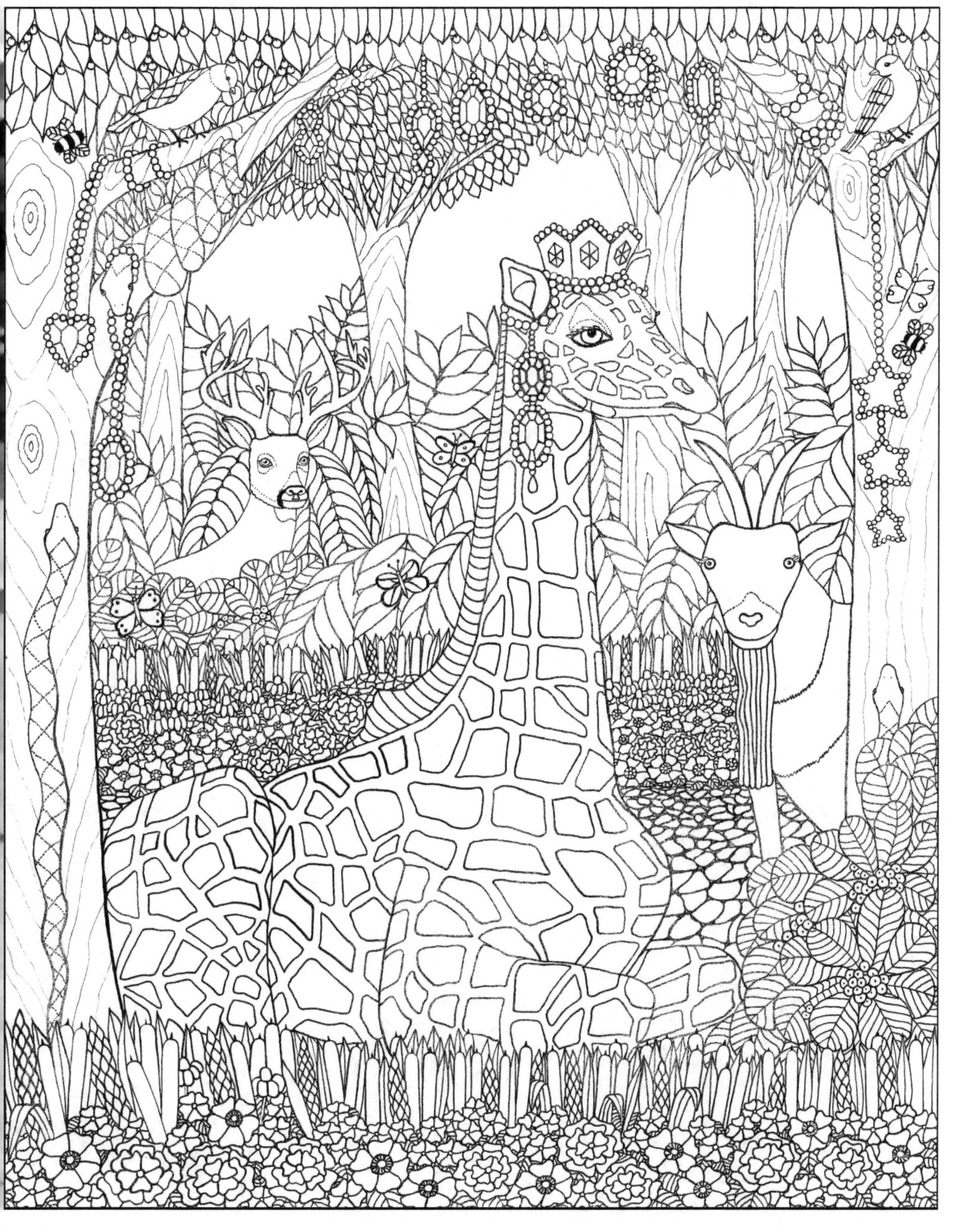

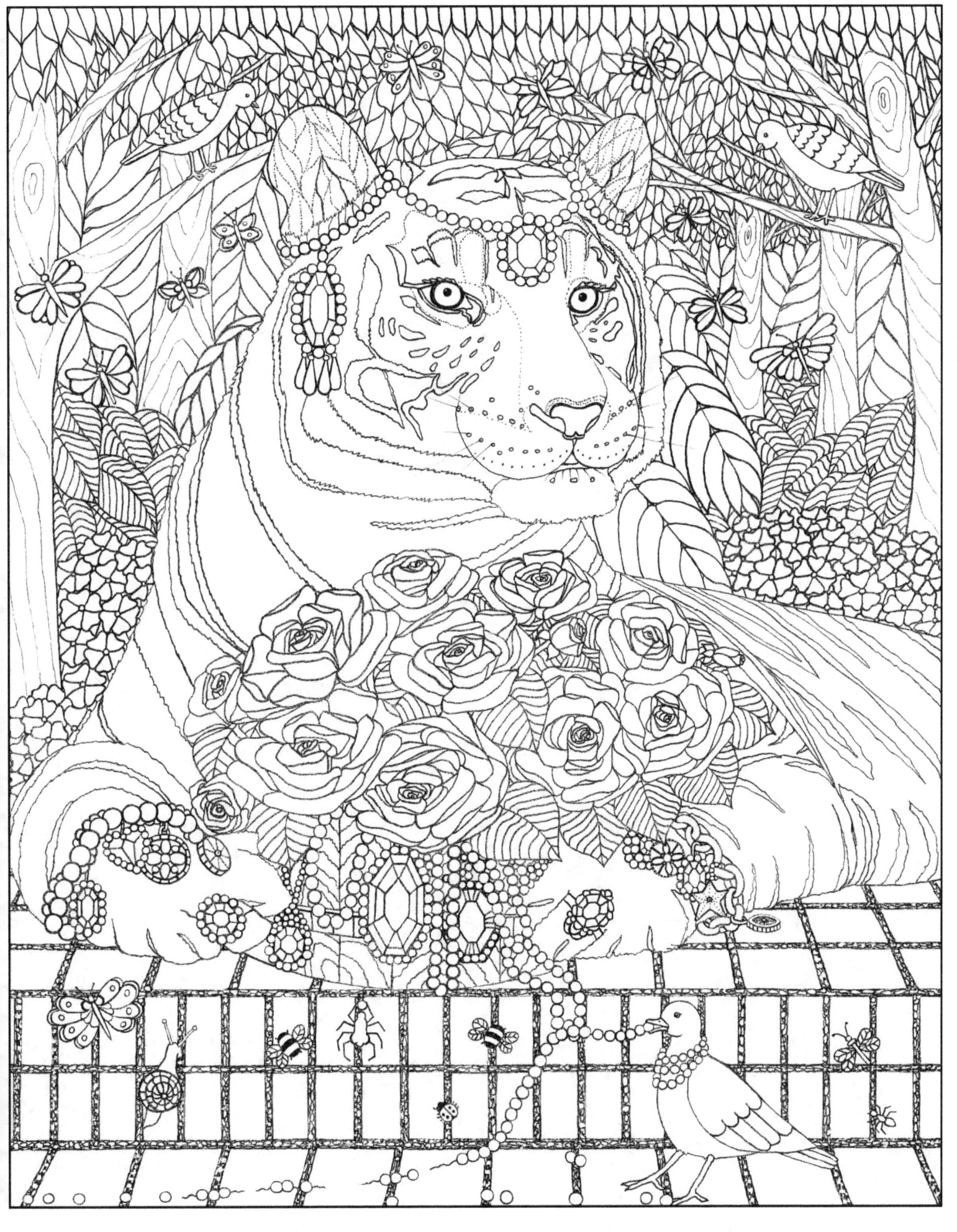

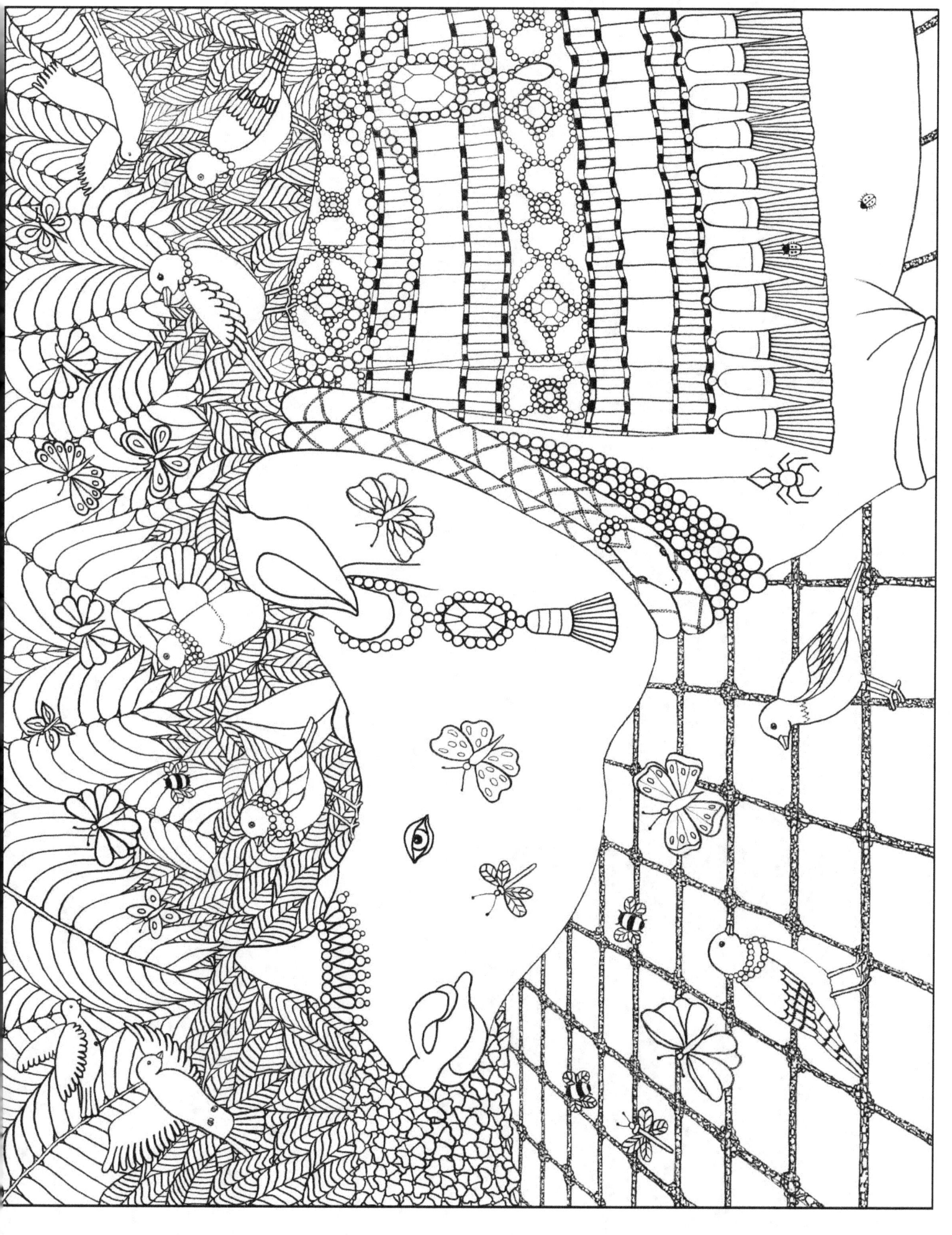

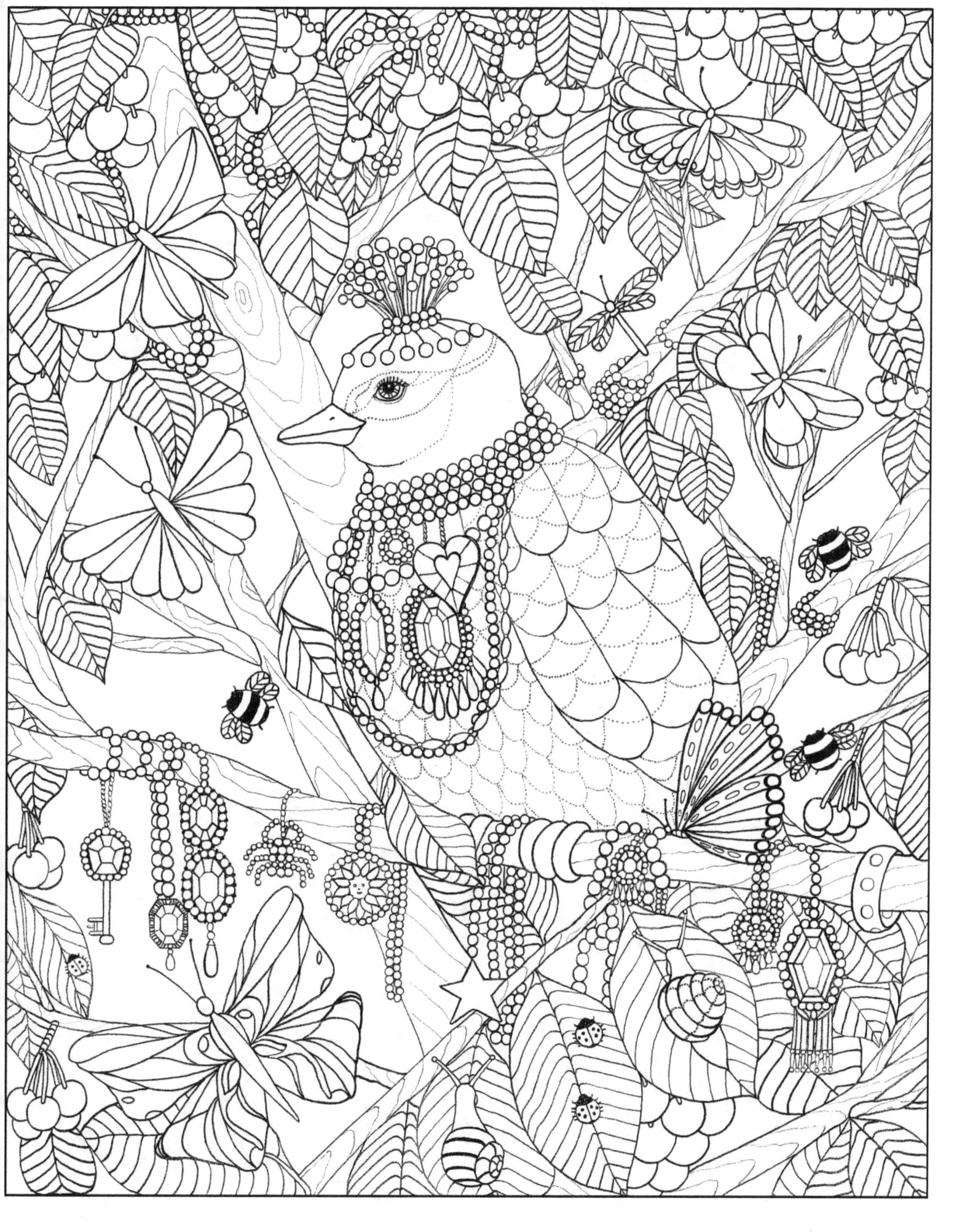

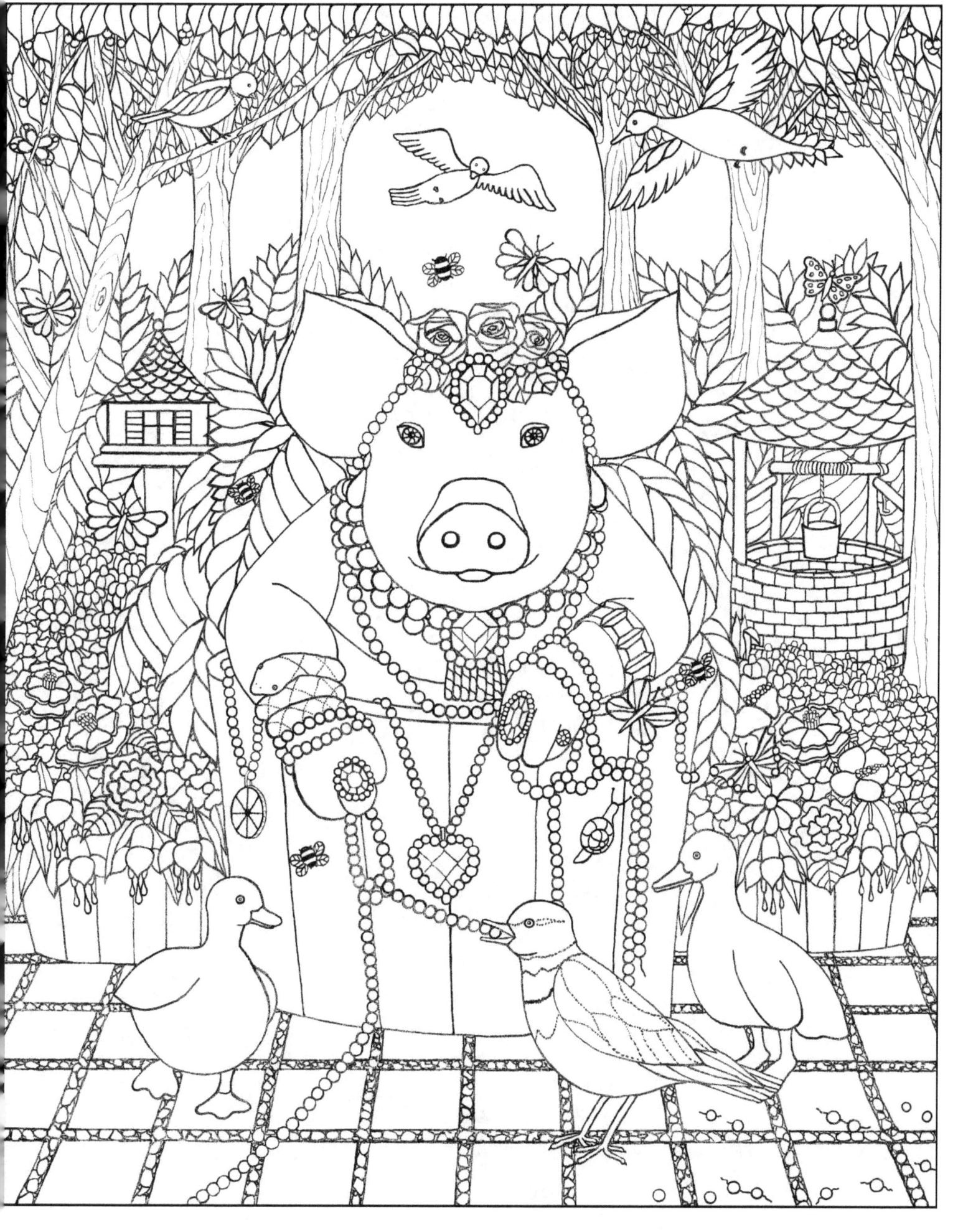

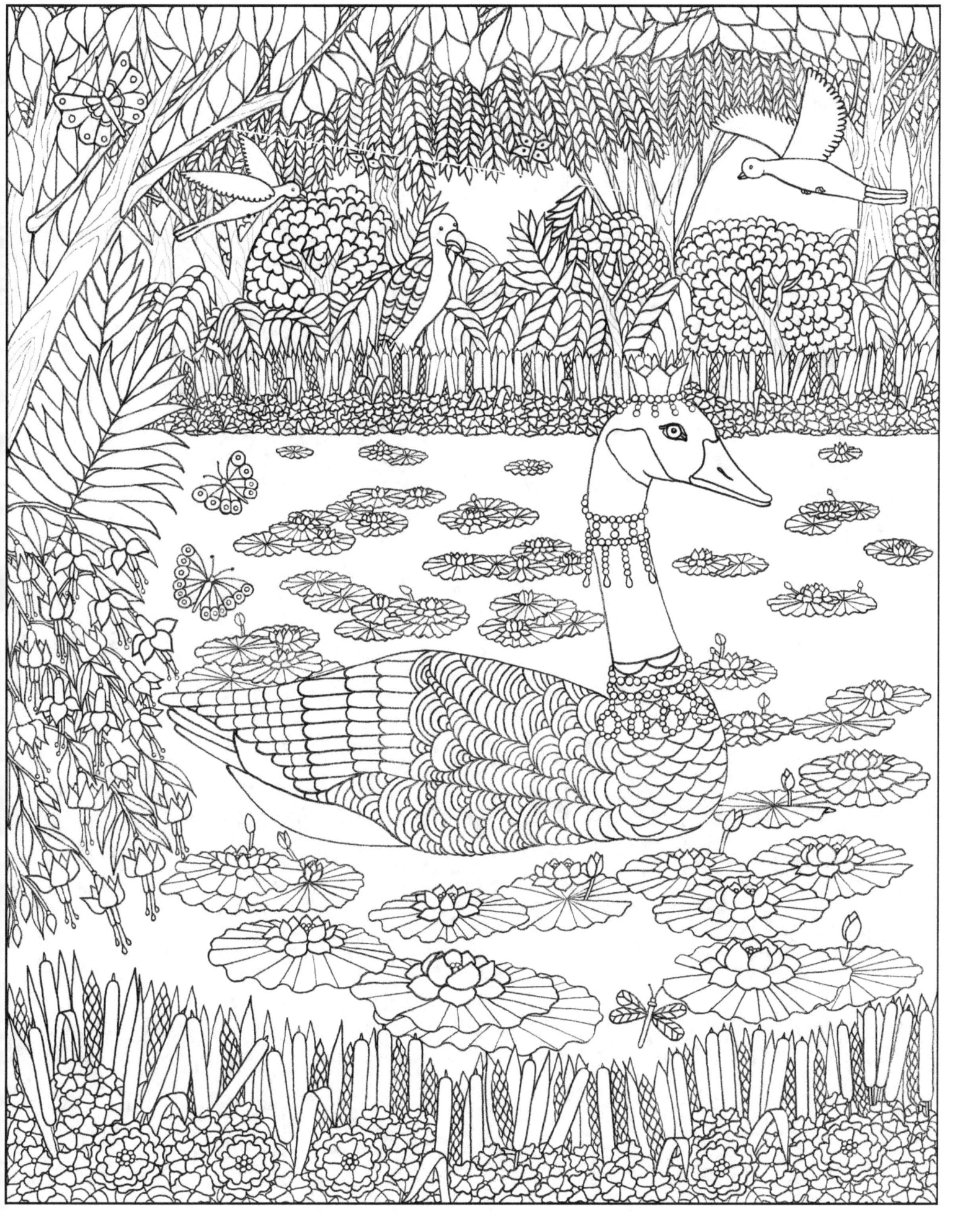

The End